FIRING DAYS

FIRING DAYS

Reminiscences of a
Great Western Fireman

by
Harold Gasson

Oxford Publishing Co · Oxford

© 1973 Oxford Publishing Co.

Reprinted 1974
Reprinted 1975
Reprinted 1976
Reprinted 1978

ISBN 0 902888 25 0

Source of Illustrations
All photographs by Maurice Earley and the author unless otherwise credited.

Photo Reproduction by
Oxford Litho Plates Ltd.

Printed in the City of Oxford by
B.H. Blackwells (Printing) Ltd.

Published by

Oxford Publishing Co.
8 The Roundway, Risinghurst
Headington, Oxford.

Foreword

This Book is an attempt to re-capture the happy days of Steam. I was fortunate enough to serve with a most Honourable Company of Gentlemen — the Enginemen and Shed Staff of Didcot Locomotive Department.

During the 1939-45 War, Didcot, as a Main Line Shed in the London Division, was in a unique position. The locomotives of all the other Companies, including the U.S.A. Army Transportation Corps, were serviced and worked by Didcot Enginemen. After working these 'foreign locomotives' we were delighted to find that a fact was confirmed, we were indeed working on "God's Wonderful Railway".

The locomotives of Messrs. Webb, Churchward, Collett, and Hawksworth were the finest in the world.

Didcot Locomotive Shed is now a living Steam Museum, but it is with pleasure I find that the Great Western Preservation Society have re-captured the atmosphere of a past age, even to including 6106 Tank, an original locomotive stationed at Didcot during my cleaning and firing days.

H.H. Gasson. 1973

DIDCOT, NEWBURY, SOUTHAMPTON LINE

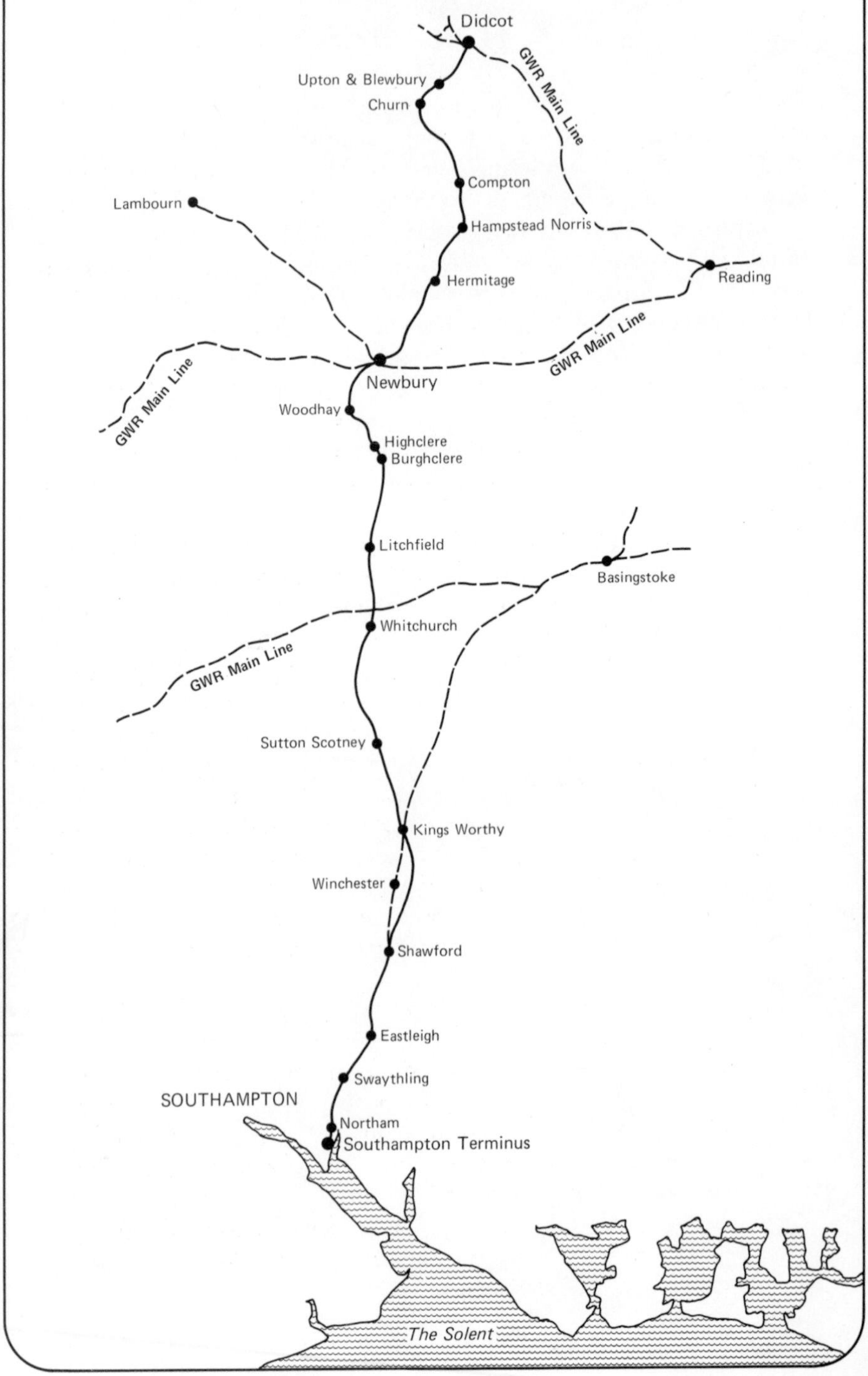

Didcot

GWR Main Line

Upton & Blewbury

Churn

Compton

Lambourn

Hampstead Norris

Reading

Hermitage

GWR Main Line

GWR Main Line

Newbury

Woodhay

Highclere

Burghclere

Litchfield

Basingstoke

Whitchurch

GWR Main Line

Sutton Scotney

Kings Worthy

Winchester

Shawford

Eastleigh

Swaythling

SOUTHAMPTON

Northam

Southampton Terminus

The Solent

I

Early Days

My introduction to the Great Western Railway steam locomotives at Didcot and my subsequently joining the ranks of the enginemen working those engines all started through a chain of events begun by my Aunt Annie in 1905. Annie Gasson lived in a farm cottage with her parents, four brothers, and two sisters. The cottage was situated in the small hamlet of Charcotte, just outside Tonbridge.

As was expected of young girls in those day, she left home and entered 'service' and by 1910 she had obtained a position of Cook to a household in the Banbury Road, Oxford. While working in this house she was to meet a young man who was to become her whole life until she died in July 1972. This young man was working as an Engine Cleaner at Oxford Locomotive Shed at this time, and was one Albert Edmonds, normally known as Bert. His journey to and from the shed took him up and down the Banbury Road twice each day, and with an eye for a pretty girl it was not long before he spotted Annie, and being an enterprising young man, as were all Great Western Cleaners, he took steps to make her acquaintance at St. Giles' Fair. That they were made for each other was evident from the start, for the courtship blossomed. Annie took what was later to prove a vital step in my life; she took Bert home to meet the family, where he was accepted with open arms. What his thoughts were of the South Eastern and Chatham Railway between Reading and Penshurst Station as he, a Great Western man, made the journey with Annie are not recorded, but the locomotives must have made a profound impression, as we shall see.

After the introductions had been made, and Bert settled in, Annie did not see a lot of him for the rest of that weekend, as two of her brothers, William and Harold, found that they had a lot in common with him. They were both spellbound by Bert's description of the Great Western Railway, and any comment of the South Eastern and Chatham was quickly dismissed in true Great Western pride. Bert talked long and ardently about Armstrong and Webb engines, and particularly about Mr. Churchward's three French engines at Oxford, 102 *La France*, 103 *President*, and 104 *Alliance*.

After Bert and Annie had returned to Oxford, Bill and Harold started to take more interest in the local railway. On the way to work they had to go through the level crossing at Penshurst Station, and up to this point they had considered it an inconvenience to be held up by the locked gates; they would pass the time of day with 'Old Joe' the Signalman, but never take much notice of the locomotives. However, Bert's visit had changed all that. They began to take an almost professional interest in the 4–4–0 Jumbo's, 0–6–0 Stirlings, and the tall chimney 0–4–4 Tanks.

There were long conversations in bed until the small hours, about railway work, then Dad Gasson told them to shut up and go down to Tonbridge Shed in the morning and try their luck, as it was quite evident now that neither of them were going to muck out cow sheds, milk cows, or scare crows much longer.

They cycled into Tonbridge to have a look, but there was no *La France* on Tonbridge Shed. Bert had done his work well; the seeds of future Great Western Enginemen had been sown, and were soon to bear fruit. They both decided that a better and more exciting life lay in the direction of Oxford, so they promptly packed their few possessions together and set off. The South Eastern and Chatham's loss was to be the Great Western's gain, as both lads were to have a long and distinguished career as members of an elite group of men on the locomotive staff of 'God's Wonderful Railway'. They set off from Penshurst Station in the late afternoon on a Sunday, changing at Redhill for Reading, which landed them up at the terminus of the South Eastern. At Reading General they found that the last train to Oxford had gone, so after a meal and a walk round the town, they returned to the station to await the first morning train. It never occurred to either of them that Reading might have a locomotive shed; all they could think about was Oxford and all those engines that Bert had talked about. At 4.00am a kindly Guard gave them a lift to Oxford on a milk empty, where they arrived in time for a quick wash in the toilet. Bert had talked about 6.00am start, no hardship for two farm boys, but they didn't want to arrive late, even if there was no job waiting for them.

At 6.00am, with no job, little money, and that queasy feeling in the stomach, they knocked on the door of 'Jobber Brown' the Foreman of Oxford Locomotive Shed.

At the curt bid to enter, they took a deep breath and walked in to meet a most formidable man wearing the Great Western badge of office, the bowler hat.

The fact that Harold could charm the birds off a tree, and that Bill could take over when his brother dried up, coupled with Bert Edmond's name, must have impressed Mr. Brown. Here in his office he had two lads, who had scorned the South Eastern and Chatham, and had come all the way from Kent to join the Great Western at Oxford, and what's more, they could tell him why it had to be the Great Western and no other.

'Jobber' did not relish the idea of refusing them a chance to become members of his staff, so he sent them to see Mr. Swallow the Foreman Cleaner. This gentleman found he had on his hands a situation that he was unprepared for, but he, too, was impressed by the two lads and their story, so he solved the problem in the one way he knew how. While he collected his thoughts together, he gave them a large cardboard box full of lengths of coloured wool and told them to sort the wool out into piles of the same colour. He said he would return later to see how they were getting on.

What this could have to do with steam engines neither could figure out, but with Father's advice to keep their eyes open and mouths shut they got on with the job.

The difficulty was that so many predecessors had handled the wool with grubby fingers that the colours were much about the same. However, small piles of wool began to grow larger on the table. They were not to know that this was the Great Western's way of testing for colour blindness, a method which was to continue for a long time to come.

Mr. Swallow returned, looked at the piles of wool, then swept them all back into the cardboard box. He gave them an envelope addressed to a Doctor in High Street, and told them to report there at 10.00am for a medical examination. This Doctor was the medical officer retained by the Great Western to deal with staff when they arrived in the Oxford area. They both had a stiff medical examination; (as Bill said "for everything except Foot and Mouth!"). One thing which did puzzle them for a time was when they were both given a glass jar and instructed to fill it with water. In vain they looked round for a tap, until the Doctor informed them in no uncertain terms on how to fill the jars! However, they were sent back to the Loco Shed with the news that they had passed.

For a second time that day they knocked on 'Jobber Brown's' door. Mr. Brown read the contents of the envelope they had brought back from the Doctor, and with a smile told them that they were both accepted as Cleaners and could start next morning, but in the meantime they should have a look round the Shed and meet some of the other Cleaners.

As it was now mid-day there were not many engines on Shed except those in the boiler washout, but to the brothers' delight 102 *La France* was one of them. No thoughts were given to clothing as they clambered aboard her, where they found everything Bert had told them was true. Gleaming copper pipes, brass fittings, and that wonderful aroma of steam, hot oil, and the quiet gentle noise of a large steam engine at rest.

A very loud shout aroused them from their day-dreaming, with the firm order to get down from that so and so engine. It was 'Old Swallow', as they were to get to know him. They came down as ordered, and were promptly told to get back up again and this time to come down the right way. They did not know, of course, that to come down from the footplate with their backs to the steps was not only almost impossible but highly dangerous.

Mr. Swallow then took them round the Shed, explaining the duties of a Cleaner and the need to be at all times punctual, obedient, and sober; he then went on to explain that they would receive 12/0d a week for a twelve hour day, working six days a week alternating with a twelve hour night duty. Sunday would be a day off, and he expected to see them in church.

Lodgings had been found for them in Hythe Bridge Street at 11/6d a week, so in their wisdom the Great Western had made sure of two things; they would surely remain sober on sixpence a week pocket money, and would not lead a riotous life so far from home.

Bill and Harold soon settled down to the life of a Cleaner, and as members of a regular gang they became adept with scrapers, tallow, and cleaning rags. Each gang of half a dozen lads were allocated several locomotives which became their responsibility, so there was much rivalry between gangs as to who had the cleanest engine.

Bill and Harold had 103 *President* as the "number one engine", but, such was the standard of cleaning, there was not much to choose between any of the engines on Oxford Shed; in any case, 'Old Swallow' saw to that.

Mr. Swallow was a good Foreman Cleaner. His standards of cleanliness took on an elaborate form of inspection, whereby he would produce from his pocket a steel foot rule which he would poke between the frames, and then would wipe the rule on a clean piece of linen; if this showed any trace of grime Mr. Swallow would show his displeasure in the form of a fine, usually a half-hour loss of pay, so on a pay rate of 12/0d there were some very clean engines! A cabin was provided for meal breaks, known as 'The Black Hole' (a term that needs no description), but the day shift were far too busy to use it, and the night shift found that an empty firebox with a flare lamp perched on the brick arch was a safe place to disappear for the odd half an hour.

They both, of course, saw a lot of Bert and Annie, but Bert did confess that life was a little difficult for a few weeks until Annie had got over the shock of Bill and Harold turning up in Oxford. With Annie a Cook in a big house, food was no problem, and they were the best fed lads in the Shed.

A very happy year passed, then Bert's expected promotion to Fireman came up, which meant a move from Oxford as he was posted to the Main Line Shed at Cardiff. It was time for a wedding, so all four of them went home to Penshurst for a week.

As they walked up the wooden platform at Penshurst Station and passed the engine, Bill and Harold had some very caustic remarks to make about the South Eastern and Chatham loco stock but, as Bert could see the fireman reaching for a coal pick, he very wisely kept his mouth shut.

The wedding took place in the little church just up the hill from the station, and in a way it was a true railway wedding, because as they waited to go over the level crossing a 'Jumbo' came by and gave them a blast on the whistle; the gesture returned by Bill and Harold gave no doubt that a Western whistle would have been preferred.

Bert and Annie left for Cardiff at the end of the week, and Bill and Harold prepared to return to Oxford. When their train ran into Penshurst they both crept into the coach without any comment about South Eastern Locomotives, for it was the same crew that had brought them down and discretion was the order of the day.

They started back on the night shift and were in trouble at once through a silly prank. All Cleaners get up to some kind of mischief, but this one is still remembered by some of the retired Enginemen at Oxford. In Hythe Bridge Street some few houses up from their lodgings lived a gentleman whose occupation was to convey cakes from a famous Oxford cake maker to the Station. His transport for this job was a box tricycle, and to allow him to make an early start he would ride the machine home at night, parking it outside his house.

In the early hours of the Tuesday morning following their return, Bill and Harold 'borrowed' thirty feet of old signal wire, then crossed the main line, went through the Midland Railway Yard and the Oxford Coal Yard and out into Hythe Bridge Street, where they proceeded to wire the tricycle's pillar to a nearby lamp-post.

Soon after 6.00am all the night shift lads, and some of the day shift, were gathered just round the corner of the coal yard, looking up Hythe Bridge Street waiting to see the fun. Sure enough the inevitable happened. The portly gentleman came out of his front door, with great ceremony placed his cycle clips in position, and mounted the tricycle. They thought for a moment that he had noticed the wire; but portly gentlemen do not just ride off – there was a period of adjustment. Then he set off down the slight fall of the road towards them, with the wire uncurling behind him, and by the time he had travelled the thirty feet he was going a fair old lick.

He came to a very sudden stop, (in railway circles it is known as a 'rough shunt'); he sailed over the top of the tricycle, still in a sitting position, and landed in the middle of the wet coal slurry and cart ruts in the gate-way of the coal yard.

There was a mad scramble, reminiscent of a rugby forward line on the move, back to the safety of the Shed but Bill and Harold were recognised. They sat in the 'Black Hole' for an hour waiting for things to settle down, then crept back to their lodgings. At 9.00am a day shift Cleaner fetched them out of bed, with orders to report to Mr. Brown within the hour. As they walked to the Shed both discussed the possibility of dismissal, and the shame of returning home, so it was with a tremulous feeling that they knocked on the office door.

Mr. Brown was waiting, sitting behind his desk, with Mr. Swallow at his side; both gentlemen were wearing their bowler hats, so Bill and Harold knew this was the moment of truth. A complaint had been received from that most eminent of persons, 'a Member of the Public' against the Great Western Railway, dishonour had been brought to the Locomotive Shed by two young ruffians, and the punishment must be swift and severe.

They stood there and took it all, not saying a word, as did Mr. Swallow, but both lads noticed that 'Jobber' had some trouble in keeping a stern expression on his face. They were fined one loss of duty, being told not to report that night, while the rest of the nightshift would lose one hour. They said "Thank you very much

Sir, it won't happen again Sir, we are very sorry Sir, three bags full Sir," (well, almost the last phrase), and with gratitude in their hearts backed out of the office. As they closed the door, thankful for getting off so lightly, they heard an explosion of laughter from inside the office, but they did agree on one thing – no more interviews of that nature again, the only misdeanours to arise would be the night swimming in the canal behind the Shed.

In the summer of 1915 they were promoted to Firemen at Didcot, and this association with Didcot Enginemen was to last many years. Mr. Brown and Mr. Swallow saw them on their last day at Oxford, and said that they were two of the best lads they had had through their hands; but then they said that to every Cleaner when the time came to leave. Although both gentlemen were strict and insisted on a job well done, they were sentimentalists at heart. Bill and Harold left Oxford with a clean record, and the incident with the tricycle was not recorded; it certainly would not be forgotten, but added to the folklore that builds up over the years as a little bit of the history of Oxford Shed.

At Didcot they found lodgings at the March Bridge Cottages, with Mrs. Keats, a war widow. The cottage was opposite the bridge itself, which carries the main line from Paddington to Bristol and South Wales; indeed, their bedroom window was the same level as the rails.

Bert and Annie were notified of the move, and as Bert was now firing on the vacuum fitted goods and the occasional South Wales expresses, a 'Crow' (four short and one long blast on the whistle) was a signal that he was on his way through. There was no mistaking Bert on the footplate, even when he was promoted to Driver. He was a well known figure, with a red handkerchief tied cowboy fashion round his neck and a briar pipe permanently in his mouth. If that pipe was smoking well, then so was the chimney; it only went out when Bert was having a rough trip for steam.

The lodgings with Ada Keats turned out to be a real home from home, particularly in Bill's case, as he became very attached to Ada. She responded likewise so they decided to get married. Harold moved on to other lodgings and settled down with Jackie Wilkins, a well known and respected Driver in the Didcot passenger link, and remained there until he too gave up the batchelor's life in 1922.

In 1924 I arrived as his only son, and much to his dismay, Mother registered me with the local authority with the same name of Harold. She waited until he was on a double home turn to do it, so the foul deed was over when he arrived back home. He hated the name to such an extent I can never remember him using it; it was always 'mate' or 'son'.

Two Harolds in the household was a bit confusing at times, especially when visitors were present, so Mother arrived at a typical woman's solution, Harold number one became Big Harold, Harold number two became Little Harold. The 'Little' bit stuck to me, even when I topped the old chap by a good six inches.

Bill and Harold were on the long slow haul through the links, which were in effect a prolonged apprenticeship to the status of Driver before I began to appreciate that my Dad was someone special.

As a very small boy, I can remember Mother taking me to the Hagbourne road bridge to see Big Harold come down the bank from Newbury with his Driver, Jim Brewer, on 3454 'Skylark' of the Bulldog class, and visits to the old wooden Shed that stood at the top of the steps which now lead to the present Shed. In 1930 engines began to take hold of me.

There was no collecting names and numbers, that was for amateurs, for I had access to the real thing. In a railway town there was no status at school in being a footplateman's son, but there was considerable rivalry between the Traffic and Locomotive Departments, so the Great Western was well equipped for future recruits.

The house seemed always full at weekends with locomen; on Sundays mornings it was Mutual Improvement Classes in the front parlour, so I was on familiar terms with eccentric rods, lifting links, lap and lead; and in the afternoon it was band practice. Dad loved music, he was a cornet player of some repute, and as Didcot Silver Band was made up almost exclusively of railwaymen, I soon knew every member of Didcot Loco Shed.

About this time, Bill and Harold moved up into the double home link, so I did not see much of either of them, as they were always in bed or away from home. In common with most Western Sheds, Didcot men's working was similar to the spokes of a wheel. They went north to Wolverhampton and Birmingham via Stratford or Banbury, East to Paddington, West to Swindon and Gloucester, and South to Westbury via Reading, and to Southampton over the Didcot-Newbury Branch. They spent two years doing this, then both moved up into the passenger link as Passed Firemen.

This was the time I really began to enjoy steam, as Big Harold was now doing driving duties from time to time. He still had a regular driver, and a regular engine, 3454 *Skylark* of my early years.

One Sunday morning in 1932 he was Shed Pilot Driver, shunting engines from the Ash Road and Coal Stage, turning them, and placing them in the Shed in the order of dispatch. The Shed was brand new, and it was arranged that I should visit it at 10.00am and spend the rest of the turn with Dad.

Builders' materials were still laid about, but what a change from the gloomy old wooden Shed. This was a day I shall never forget, for I really worked that morning, up and down from engine to engine, but the highlight came in the early afternoon, when we had to turn *Skylark*. She was standing just inside the Shed on No. 1 road, and I was allowed to drive her. I backed her gently over the points, wound the reversing lever into forward gear while Big Harold turned the points, then drove her down to the turn-table. We had her balanced so finely that I could move her unaided; then I drove her back up past the lifting shop and shed offices, over No. 1 points again and back to stop near the sand drier. There I had a surprise, as waiting to prepare her for a Sunday passenger working was Dad's regular driver, Joe Beckenham.

Joe Beckenham was a typical example of the Great Western passenger driver, being rather small in stature and inclined to stoutness, wearing clean overalls bleached almost white, with brass buttons and shoes sparkling, a heavy white moustache, rosy complexion, cap-peak polished, and a Gold Albert across his stomach; in fact, the very essence of the top link driver. He climbed up on the foot-plate, and with great ceremony placed on my head a new Engineman's cap. This cap, I believe, was the last issue to carry on each side of the peak the two small brass buttons showing, in relief, *Lord of the Isles*. The cap is long worn out of course, but I still have those two buttons in my collection of Great Western treasures, one up I think on Swindon Museum, as I have looked there in vain for replicas.

All this fun had to come to an end when Bill and Harold were made Drivers, as Bill was sent to Aberbeeg, the main Shed in the South Wales Western Valleys, which handled all the coal traffic there, and Big Harold was sent to Moat Lane Shed in Mid Wales for the summer service.

In the summer of 1933 they both had another move, Bill to Barry Dock Shed, and Harold to the Neath and Brecon Shed. Both thought at the time that the move was to be permanent, so the families were move to South Wales, but, as an insurance, both applied for a return to the London Divison, with Didcot as first choice and Reading as second.

By a twist of fate, just as the two families settled in Wales, Bert and Annie moved to Acton. Bert was promoted to Driver at Old Oak Common Shed, so he now found himself on the right hand side of the 'Twenty-Nines' and 'Castles'. The change for Bert was one of Sheds, more than of work, as his knowledge of the main line between Paddington, Bristol, and South Wales was considerable, so he soon found himself on the 'runners' again, the only difference being that he now had a chance to handle a 'King'.

Bert Edmonds and a 'King' in good order were a formidable combination. He soon became known as a member of a small group of men who had that little extra which enabled them to get the best out the 'King' Class in the most adverse conditions. I've seen him go through Didcot and down Savernake Bank doing the magic Ton, and he didn't exactly hang about on the 'Castles'. Like Bill and Harold, he was loved by the Firemen, always taking a turn on the shovel, and never expecting a Fireman to do more than he was prepared to do himself.

During this time I did not see much of engines, except for one visit to Neath and Barry Dock Shed. Somehow this seemed different from the brand new Shed I had known at Didcot, and I suppose I was too busy growing up in a strange environment. But in 1936 everything changed again.

The long arm of 'Jobber Brown' reached out over the years and touched Bill and Harold. On that first day long ago he decided that as Bill was the eldest by one year, he would be senior, so when a vacancy came up in the London Division, Bill filled it. This was at Reading, which was to be the last move, and within a month a vacancy arose at Didcot which brought Harold back home again. Both brothers had been happy in South Wales and were prepared to see their time out in the Valleys, but their wives could not settle down so it was back to old friends again. Harold was most upset, not that he didn't welcome the return to his old Shed, but he loved the Welsh people, and nothing pleased him more in later years when I met and married a girl from those same Valleys.

As a child I had spend odd weekends back where it had all begun at Charcotte. This was a wonderful place to go to, as when one left Penshurst Station to reach the cottage, the footpath led across the perimeter of the aerodrome, where flying was always in progress. The aircraft were Avros and Sopwiths, and the pilot would give a friendly wave to a small boy as he swished overhead, with magnetos cut and engine spluttering, to make a bumpy landing on the grass.

During the period spent in South Wales the annual one week's holiday was spent at Charcotte. I was now old enough to take interest in the 'other railway' and its locomotives, and I cultivated the friendship of the Signalman at Penshurst Box. The amount of different engines passing up and down between Redhill and Tonbridge was amazing. There were engines of all shapes and sizes and there was nothing standard as I was used to seeing on the Western. I spent hours in that small signal box, and looking back on it now I can see that my friend the Signalman was very indulgent to the critical remarks I made about what was by now the Southern Railway; very bad manners on my part, but such is the way of inexperienced youth.

There was plenty of leg-pulling from Grandad Gasson about how there was one more future professional water boiler in the family, but he was a grand old man who never showed his disappointment in the fact that only one son stopped on the farm. He would talk about how he remembered his grandfather living in the cottage, so quite a few small Gassons had trod the brick path up to the front door.

The rest of his family were connected with railways, as the two remaining girls had married Southern men — Elsie was married to George Young, a goods Guard at Tonbridge, and Mabel was married to Fred Holman, Signalman at Minster — so the topic of conversation at the table was certainly not about heifers or milk yields.

His youngest son, Arthur, was a disappointment to us, although he thought he had the best job out of all the Gasson Clan. He was a Green Line bus driver, which he said was the only job to sort out the men from the boys; this statement only came when he was on his way out through the door. How can a petrol engine compare with Steam? Ugh . . .

Dad told me once that the Valleys were very much like working the Didcot to Winchester Branch, except that whereas he could spell Upton, Compton, etc, the Welsh names had him beat. However, at Moat Lane and at Neath he had Welsh-speaking Firemen, so he was able to manage.

Bill's move to Reading was the result of a retirement, but Harold's came as a result of a tragic accident, which lead to the

11

death of a brother-engineman, Ernest Edmonds. Ernie was a well-loved and respected man, he was a local J.P., an Alderman, and the branch secretary of the A.S.L.E.&F. He was preparing a 'Dean Goods', and had just got up between the front of the firebox behind the big ends to remove the corks for oiling, when a 'Bulldog' in front moved back a few inches and buffered up to Ernie's engine. The big ends moved, and crushed Ernie. His injuries were too severe for him to recover. It was an accident that affected me also, as I had known Ernie Edmonds since I was a very small child, and I had never given it a thought that my beloved engines could hurt anyone.

Now that Harold was back, I started where I had left off, spending every Saturday or Sunday on the footplate when he was on a local shunting job. Looking back over the years I wonder how I ever got away with it, as I never once saw a Foreman; there are two possibilities — they either kept out of the way as they could see a future engineman, or, the 'old chap' took care to see that I was only allowed on the Shed when no Foreman was about. All I know is that I had the time of my life, and couldn't wait until I was old enough to officially join the Great Western.

I had to wait until I was sixteen, however, so I filled in the time after leaving school as a messenger boy at R.A.F. Benson, starting at 6.45am after a ten mile cycle ride, which was at least good training for getting up in the morning. One thing struck me as ironic about the job; I was paid 12/0d a week, not much progress from Bill and Harold in 1910, and although Fairey Battles and Hampdens had a certain amount of glamour, they didn't work by steam, and certainly were not worth twelve bob a week with a twenty mile ride thrown in. My sixteenth birthday came in August 1940, and in early September I received a letter to report to Park House, Swindon, for an examination for Locomotive Cleaner. Eureka! Here I come at last!

2

Cleaning Days

On September 6th 1940 I stood at Didcot Station on the Down Main Platform opposite West End Signal Box, waiting for the 5.30am Paddington. I had a free pass in my pocket made out to one H.H. Gasson, Didcot to Swindon Return. My orders were to report to Park House at 9.00am, and I did not intend to be late.

It was a typical September morning – thick fog, with the promise of a fine day. Fog held no problems for a train starting only 53 miles away with A.T.C. to guide it, and right on time 6026 *King John* rolled in and stopped near me. I could hear the "whoosh" of the vacuum brake as she came to a stand, and as I opened the carriage door, the large ejector was opened up to blow the brakes off again. At last I was on my way to join the two gentlemen up front. It was 6.40am and we were away, clearing the fog at Challow, so when I arrived at Swindon I had plenty of time for a cup of tea before walking down the road. When I arrived at Park House I found only two lads there, but by 8.30 our total had grown to seven, and, with the familiarity of boys forced with each others company, we soon knew all about one anothers' hopes and fears. The Woodbines were handed round and with the nervousness we all felt it did not take long to fill up the ash tray. Out of the seven, one other lad had railway connections as I did. His father was a Driver at Severn Tunnel Loco Shed so with this common bond the two of us were a little condescending to the others.

At 9.00am the examination started, with some simple arithmetic and dictation. We were then given the Medical such as Bill and Harold experienced 30 years before; it was as Bill had said, for everything except Foot and Mouth, but when given the glass jar and told to fill it with water, I did not look for a tap. Such is progress. When this was all over and we were dressed again, we were taken to another room for the eyesight test. This was something we were familiar with at school – the card on the wall, first cover the right eye, then the left; but it was not to end there, for a cardboard box was brought in and placed on the table. This was a very old box, patched all round the corners with medical tape, and on the side, almost faded away with age, was the crayoned word, "Oxford". Inside this battered old box was the most motley collection of coloured wool I have ever seen.

I burst out laughing and was very sharply informed that it was no laughing matter, for this was a serious examination to determine if I could distinguish one colour from another, and particular attention would be taken over my selection.

My little pile of coloured wool was examined piece by piece, then put back into the box which was taken out, to disappear from my life for ever. Could it have been the same box of wool Bill and Harold had gone through 30 years before?

We were told to settle down for ten minutes, so out came the Woodbines again while we held an inquest on our possible progress. We just had time to suck them down before the door opened, and the Severn Tunnel lad and myself were summoned to another room.

The gentleman who sat behind the desk was the same person who had conducted the wool test. On the coat hanger was a bowler hat, so we both knew we were in the presence of a man of some consequence. He informed us that out of the seven lads examined, we were the only two who had passed. He then enquired into my disgraceful behaviour during the test, so I told him the story about Bill and Harold. This caused as much merriment on his part as it had on mine, and he had to agree that it could be the same box of wool, as he had been using it for years. Seven years later, Bill's son, Ted, followed my footsteps to Park House, and he too found that a battered old cardboard box full of wool was still in use.

There should be a place of honour in Swindon Museum for that cardboard box; it must be one of the original relics of the Great Western Railway Locomotive Examination Board.

So I was through, with orders to report at Didcot Loco Shed for cleaning duties on Monday, September 27th 1940.

That first morning I walked through the station subway, up the steps and down the cinder path by the coal stage excited by the thought that in a few minutes I would be climbing all over steam engines, and getting paid for it. However, I was quickly disillusioned when I reported to Ernie Didcock, the Chargehand Cleaner.

In the chain of command from Cleaner to Shed Foreman I was right at the bottom, so for starters I could clean out the ashes and light the fire in the Foreman's office. Disposing of ashes was no problem — one simply tipped the bucket onto the nearest pile of locomotive ashes — and filling the bucket with coal was not a challenge to your ingenuity for you climbed up one-handed on to the nearest engine and filled the bucket. I found that it was not easy to climb down from the footplate of a Saint with a bucket of coal in one hand so, since the small Tankies carried the same brand of coal, I filled up from them without having to struggle to get down so far, and losing half the load in the process.

Once the fire was alight, I had to go into the stores and assist there, weighing up cotton waste in ¼lb balls, issuing oil to Enginemen, and generally helping to do all the hundred and one jobs in a busy locomotive shed stores.

The Storeman was Reubin Hitchman, who was the kindest of men, so my time as the junior Cleaner was spent in very pleasant company. He went out of his way to help all the lads as they passed through his hands, so that when one moved on, out into the Shed, it was an easy transition.

The night duty was one that I did enjoy, as from midnight I was out on the streets of Didcot calling up crews, (the junior Cleaner was, in fact, the call boy.) I started at 10.00pm by helping Reubin in the Stores until 11.30pm, then I copied the names of all the Drivers and Firemen who were on duty from 1.00am until 5.45am, and then the fun started. You would call in order of booking on, standing outside the customer's house shouting as loud as possible, "Driver Jones, Driver Jones", until an answer was received, and then you shouted out the duty and the time of booking on.

This was all right as long as the man concerned woke up at once, but if he was a heavy sleeper and you had to keep on calling, the neighbours got a little upset. Dad's Fireman, Bill Yaxsley was the worst one to have to wake up; I could call and call, without result, and then a neighbour would open the window and start casting doubts on my ancestry. I would abuse him back and eventually the front door would open and a strategic withdrawal had to be made — in other words, you got on your bike, and went like hell! The neighbour would then take action by getting Bill up, to stop me from returning and starting it all over again. I still see Bill and have a laugh over old times, as he now drives a stinking old diesel shunting engine for British Leyland at Cowley.

Jim Brewer, Dad's Driver of my childhood days, had a better method of being called. He had fixed up a bell push on his window-sill, which he connected to the bell on his bed headboard. It worked satisfactorily for years, until I brought some sticky tape from the first aid box with me one morning and taped the button down.

This led to my first interview with Bill Young, the Shed Foreman. Bill was a little man, never without his bowler hat, and, as we shall see later, he had a soft spot. As this was my first offence, I got off with a warning.

There were 'perks' to the callboy's job; we soon got to know which Enginemen's gardens had ripe apples and there was always the Nestles chocolate machine on number 5 platform.

The War had not been on long enough to affect supplies, so the chocolate machine was kept full. One good kick and a snatch at the draw-handle would produce a bar of chocolate every time. It was a secret handed down from callboy to callboy, and never shared with the station staff, such was the rivalry between the Locomotive Department and the Traffic Department, although we did condescend to share a pot of tea in the Porters' Room between calls. They were a good lot on the Station, but conversation was kept at a neutral level, as the rivalry between departments was something to be believed. A Southern Engineman would argue against a Western man on locomotives, but all Enginemen would close ranks against the Traffic side!

At the end of January 1941 another lad started cleaning, so I was no long the baby of the Shed, and it was time to move out of the stores.

About this time I was issued with an identification card and a brass check, two items I still have and treasure. I was one step nearer to the Main Line.

In the issue of the brass check the Great Western were very wise in the ways of Engine Cleaners. The Drivers and Firemen were gentlemen — they merely shouted to the time clerk to be booked on and that was that — but the Cleaners had to have some physical proof that they were indeed on duty, so they handed in this brass check when booking on, and collected it when booking off. The check was also used for collecting one's pay. I 'lost' my check when promoted to Fireman, but I kept it to prove that I was not a gentleman at least at one time in my life. The check measures 1in x ½in and is stamped *G.W.R. Loco. Dept.,* and in the middle is the number *262.* I was a mere number!

The identification card was issued for my protection against trigger-happy soldiers, or so we were told. It was in the days when German paratroops were landing in France dressed as nuns, so the Great Western thought they could just as easily land dressed as railwaymen. We looked to the sky for our German Cleaner — we would have been only too pleased to show him how to rake out a full engine ashpan on a windy day.

My card is 3″ x 4″, coloured pink, bears the G.W.R. badge, the number 47806, and reads thus:

> The undermentioned person is authorised to be on the Lines and Premises of the Great Western Railway Company while in the execution of his duty. This card is valid until cancelled or withdrawn.

Name in Full . . . . . Gasson Harold Henry

Department . . . . . . C M E

Grade . . . . Locomotive Cleaner/Fireman

Stationed at . . . . . DIDCOT LOCO

The Identification Card must be signed in ink by the holder immediately he receives it, and be carried by him until further notice when engaged in work on the Railway. It must be produced at any time on request, and the holder must, if required, sign his name as a proof of his identity.

To Didcot Loco I was a number, to the Manager I existed; honour was satisfied.

Cleaning engines in 1941 with the War well and truly on became very much a secondary occupation, and we Cleaners were pressed into covering every job in the Shed. There was an acute shortage of labour in those days, so we washed out boilers acting as boilersmith mates, assisted the fitters as mates, dropped fires, and coaled engines, but it was all good training in the running of a busy locomotive shed. One job we all hated was coaling engines, as it meant shovelling coal out of a 20 ton wagon into tubs, then tipping the contents of the tub into the tender waiting below. It always seemed to me that whenever I was detailed to work at the coal stage it was blowing a gale; consequently one was covered with coal dust in the first hour. One duty that gave light relief was damping down fires on the ash road. This was necessary because the glow of dropped fires during the night gave away the position of the Shed to German bombers, so a Cleaner was detailed to use a hose pipe to damp down the glowing coals as the firebox was being emptied.

The blackout was complete to such an extent that one had to use a hand lamp to get about the Shed, and poor old Jack Jacobs was no exception. He was a ponderous man, very bad on his feet, and never without his badge of office, the foreman's bowler hat. To see a hand-lamp appear from the Shed and come slowly towards one was a signal that Jack was on his way. We would judge the pace and distance, then lift the hose pipe just a fraction, and Jack would get a wet bowler every time. In the blackout he could never find the culprit.

I once received a right old wigging and the threat of being sent home, from Bill Young the Senior Foreman, for a prank I should have had more sense than to try. I was detailed to assist George Giles, the senior Boilersmith, in washing out the boiler of 'Bulldog' 3376 *River Plym*. George was in the firebox tapping stays, so I stuck a hose pipe in a tube at the smokebox end and turned the tap on! George crawled out of that firebox wet through, and proceeded to play hell. Now I had to face the music. Bill Young to his credit did not tell the 'Old Chap', but of course he soon heard of it, so I had a second session when he came home. I had the good sense not to remind him of the box cycle incident in Hythe Bridge Street years before.

A cold dismal morning in early February of 1941 found me in the fire-box of 5935 *Norton Hall* equipped with flare lamp, short pricker, and handbrush. It was not such a bad place to be as she still had 40lbs showing on the steam gauge and was pleasantly warm. She was booked in for washout and tubes, so my task was to hook the 'corks' of clinker out of the tubeplate, then brush off the brick-arch. At 7.00am I was well on my way to completion when I heard banging on the steel footplate and my name being called. I stood up, with my head and shoulders sticking out of the firebox doors to see the shift Foreman, Jack Jacobs, calling me. He informed me that the Fireman on the West End Pilot had gone home sick and I would have to take over the duty. I quickly climbed out of the firebox, handed in my tools to the Chargehand Cleaner, picked up my box from the Cleaners' cabin and made my way to Didcot West End Box. I was also careful to check the "time". This was important to a Cleaner, as, if a firing duty was 6½ hours or over this counted as a firing turn and was not only paid as such but went towards counting in seniority when one became a Fireman. The duty was booked until 2.00pm so this would be my first turn as a Fireman.

I crossed the carriage sidings, the up yard and centre yard to west yard, and there, in all her grime and glory, stood 907. Built in 1875 she still retained the open cab but had fitted to her the spark arrester chimney for working in the Didcot Ordnance Depot. To me at that moment she could have been *King George V*. I climbed aboard her and saw that my mate for the day was Joe Withers, one of the senior enginemen at Didcot and who was now on pilot driving work because of poor health. Joe was one of the true 'characters' of Didcot Shed, a very tall thin man addicted to the habit of taking snuff. Joe greeted me warmly, enquiring as to my skill in handling the shovel. I confidently assured him that I knew where the injectors were and what to do, but that morning I was to learn a great deal more of life on the footplate of a steam engine.

The steam pressure was at 100lbs so I fired her all round the box until she came round almost to her blowing off point of 165lbs. The water in the glass was thick with chalk and only about an inch was showing, so I put on the left hand injector and brought it up to three-quarters full. On Great Western pannier tank engines it was always the left hand injector which was used, simply because the water feed was up in the Fireman's corner; the right hand injector water feed was the Driver's side, also up in the corner, but young Firemen never disturbed the sanctuary of the Driver's side. I have known some Drivers draw a chalk mark down the middle of the floor boards and in such circumstances it was not wise to cross the line. Looking back over the years it would seem that the right hand injectors were as good as new because they were never used except for a test run when the engine was prepared for duty.

No. 907 was in quite a state. She smelt like a steam laundry, she also leaked steam and water from every gland, both right and left live steam unions on the injectors dripped, the regulator handle was the old single pushover type which kept up a steady weep of steam, and when a shunting movement was called for fog emerged from her leaking spindle glands. But she was my first engine and I forgave her many faults.

As I have said, Joe liked a pinch of snuff so when he offered me a pinch I accepted with innocence, always ready to try something once. Joe's idea of a pinch was a fistful and on his instruction to hold out my hand he poured on the back of it a small mountain of brown powder. I was then told to place it near my nostril and sniff hard. At that point I thought the end of the world had come; my nose was on fire, my eyes streamed, I spluttered and coughed, and in a welter of tears I filled up the bucket with cold water and stuck my head in it. I can still hear Joe's laughter, but I had learnt one lesson in life that morning — don't take up the snuff habit.

Lesson number two came soon afterwards, when Joe enquired if I had a gauge glass and rings in my box. I was proud of that box, as it was one of the genuine enginemen's boxes manufactured by Dukes of Grimsby; indeed, I still use it as a tool box. The small brass plate on it pronounced that the owner was H.H. GASSON. Inside I had my sandwiches, and a pint of cold tea in an empty whisky bottle, as this was before the days of the tea can and the footplate brew-up. As Joe had enquired about a gauge glass I slid back the small bolt of the drop-down lid. Being a keen lad I had everything, a rule book, the appendix to the rule book, a copy of Arthur Hathaway's *The Locomotive, Its Peculiarities, Failures, and Remedies,* Algy Hunt's *Descriptive Diagrams of the Locomotive,* five detonators, a red and green flag, and last but not least one gauge glass complete with two rubber rings. Joe viewed all this with quiet amusement and then enquired if I had ever changed a gauge glass. The answer was, of course, 'No'. Then to my horror Joe took of the gauge frame and calmly smashed the glass with a spanner. The result was almost indescribable as steam and water roared into the cab. I felt for the gauge frame handle, found it and shut off the steam by pulling it down, then lifted the blow-through cock. At last there was peace in the cab again, with Joe sitting on his seat taking a pinch of snuff and making comments on what a nice fine day it was to learn how to change a gauge glass.

Joe produced from his pocket a key ring which contained the wierdest collection of tools I had ever seen. All were about four inches long, made of heavy-gauge wire. There were spikes, hookers, corkscrews, and probes, everything for removing stones from horses' hoofs, and, most important, old rubber rings from gauge glass frames. It was a lesson well learnt. I was never worried about a gauge glass breaking again, for if at any time I found a suspect one on an engine it was changed at once, so I never did have one go on me when on the road. I found also that twenty Players to a Fitter was a respectable price to pay for a similar set of instruments on a key ring such as Joe had lent me on that first day as a Fireman.

Much to my delight, Joe's Fireman was off sick the rest of the week, so I had a full week of firing duties to my credit by Saturday, but not all on 907, as she was long overdue for a boiler washout, and was changed for 2076 on Wednesday. This was a far nicer engine to work on as the cab was enclosed and she was in good condition, not long back from a complete overhaul at

Swindon. It was a pleasure to brush up the new floor boards, and clean off her front boiler in the cab. With no spark arrester as with 907, and valves perfectly set, she gave out that crisp Great Western bark when moving a heavy transfer load from the centre yard, and she would steam with a candle in the firebox. It was just as well she was so free with steam, as will be seen later, for I had another reason to be grateful to that little Pannier Tank 2076.

Firing turns became more frequent now, mostly on the yard pilot duties, and of course Didcot Ordnance Depot, which was turning out vast supplies for the Army. We would book on at 4.45am for the 5.45am Depot jobs, book off Shed at 5.30am and couple up five engines at a time at the Shed signal. The Great Western had a simple system for preparing engines, from a Pannier Tank up to a Collet 22XX class. The allowance for such engines the size of 6106 Tank was three-quarters of an hour, any engine above that was allowed one hour. It was just not possible to do the preparation in the time, unless one was prepared to go off Shed half-ready, so everyone came on at least a quarter to half-hour early, if only to leave the Shed in a complete state of readiness.

The Depot engines would shunt all day returning to Shed at 6.00pm. The loaded wagons would be brought up to the hump yard for marshalling on the last trip, all five engines pushing the day's work into the Long Road, then leaving via Foxhall Junction. One engine would remain to shunt the day's work into trains ready for dispatch; this was the Hump pilot, which would pull 60 or 70 loaded wagons out of the sidings up the spur towards the rear of Foxhall box, then slowly creep back, while the shunter would uncouple for the different roads required. It was on this night Hump pilot job that I came unstuck with 2076, and it was with good reason that I was to be grateful for her steaming.

About 1.30am a goods train ran through the catch points on the up relief line at Foxhall derailing half a dozen wagons, which meant that we were blocked in until the line was clear. We had completed the work to be done at that point, so the shunters, my Driver and myself, decided to get our head down in the Shunters' cabin, an old converted coach. I filled up the boiler on 2076, shut the dampers, and then made myself comfortable with my mates, until 5.30am when the telephone rang to inform us that the line was now clear for us to leave. I climbed up on 2076, saw that we had half a glass of water, then opened the firebox doors and found that, next to dropping a lead plug, I had committed the unforgiveable sin — I had let the fire out. There was 90lbs of steam in the boiler, so I had a quick look round for anything that would burn, old bits of sleepers, branches off the trees, and grease out of the wagon axle boxes. She had been out of the Shed for 24 hours, so the firebox was full of ash and clinker, but that little engine responded splendidly to the unusual fuel, for she began to creep up on the steam gauge until I had 120lbs showing, so I was able to put on the injector and get a glass-full, but at the cost of knocking her back again to 90lbs. We crept out of the Depot with the regulator just open and with black smoke pouring out of the chimney, for all the world the first oil-burner on the Western. Foxhall Box set us for the Up Relief, which meant going through the station, instead of letting us round the West Curve; by going the latter way we could have slipped into Shed unnoticed. With our fingers crossed we made it over the points at Didcot East Junction and then we had to stop. There were 20lbs of steam on the clock when the points changed over to let us on Shed, and by all the rules 2076 should not have been able to move, but very slowly she began to creep forward, and as soon as she passed the ground frame hut she came onto the slight fall down to the ash pit. I stopped her on the handbrake, gently buffering up to the engine in front, with no steam showing on the clock. Then my mate and I gathered up our belongings and nonchalantly climbed down and walked to the Shed to book off. We kept very quiet about that incident, but somehow it got out, because for months afterwards I was constantly being offered a lighted flare lamp and the enquiry made as to my need for a light. The 'Old Chap' at home made no reference to it, other than when he had occasion to make up the fire for Mother, when he would make some very pointed remark about "keeping the home fires burning".

Poor little old 2076, I suppose she has been cut up long ago, but she remains one of the Engines I shall never forget.

The next week I was back on the Shed doing every kind of work except cleaning engines; (funnily enough I never did get to be Boilersmith's mate again — perhaps George Giles had something to do with it). Bill Miles the Senior Foreman Fitter kept me busy, and I had the job of packing the spindle glands on 907. I've no doubt that Bill had heard about the hose pipe down the tube and the "fire out" episode, but he never once mentioned it, he just kept me so busy there was no time to dwell on anything except work.

By the May of 1941 I had eighteen firing turns to my credit, all on shunting duties in either the Didcot Yards or the Ordnance

Depot, and had prepared most of the engines for those duties, so I was beginning to get the hang of things, or so I thought.

Because of War commitments there was a rapid build up of crews at Didcot. These were mostly lads from the Welsh Valleys. Firemen made up to Drivers, or Cleaners made up to Firemen, and with accommodation rather sparse in the town, they were housed in sleeping coaches stabled on the end of No. 7 and No. 8 Roads outside the Shed. A kitchen coach was also provided, with a main line chef, and this arrangement was to remain until the hostel was built. The shortage of crews was acute, and led to my first firing turn outside shunting.

As I was leaving for home one Monday afternoon, Bill Young called me into his office. As this was usually for a 'Wizzer' I tried to think back on what I should have d.. ne but hadn't or what I had done but shouldn't, but he asked me to sit down, so I knew something was on.

He then asked me if I felt ready to try a bigger firing job, so I accepted at once without question.

He explained how tight he was for crews; he had had to take a Passed Fireman off his job for a driving duty for the rest of the week, and I could take over if I felt ready for it. The Driver was willing to give me the chance, so it was up to me. The duty in question was the 7.37am Didcot to Southampton, not exactly the Torbay Express but quite an exacting task for a young Cleaner. As I left the office Bill Young's parting words were "Don't let the fire out Boyo", and as I passed his window I could see that he was grinning like a Cheshire cat; so he *had* known about that little episode with 2076.

Booking on time for the Southampton was 6.30am, off Shed at 7.15am, but I was there at 6.00am; I wanted more than three quarters of an hour to prepare an engine for this job. The engine booked was 3376 *River Plym,* a 'Bulldog'. I knew her tubes were clean as I had done them one week before, and she was tight at the front end, so I should have no trouble about steaming, and I knew I should want plenty of that before I saw the Shed again.

My Driver was Fred Essex, a man I had known all my life, and the father of one of my mates in the cleaning gang, and I was fortunate in going out with one of the kindest men it was my privilege to work with. I had known Fred as Mr. Essex for years, but he told me to cut out that nonsense; I was to refer to him as "mate", and so he was in every sense of the word.

When I climbed up on 3376, she was just right for preparing, with a nice bit of fire in the firebox, half a glass of water in the boiler, and 80lbs. on the clock, so I could spread the fire over the box and build it up without using the blower. As engine preparation is a team job, I filled the oil feeder for Fred and placed it on top of the boiler to warm; then when he went under the motion, he would check the ashpan for me — little things that made the job so much more pleasant.

I went round the framing, checking the sand box on the left hand side, then opened the smoke box, found all the plates secure, tightened the smoke box again and swept off the ashes with the hand brush, then round the right hand side to the other sand box, then back to the footplate.

While I had been busy with this Fred had arrived, collected the oil cans, drawn his requirements from the stores, and was on the footplate to greet me. He thanked me for filling his feeder and said he would check the ashpan, and if I would pull the sand levers he would check the pipes. I was off to a good start. By the time I had the fire made up well and the coal broken up and stacked on the tender, the footplate was almost clean, so I had a look over the side to see where Fred was. He was up front oiling the front coupling of the side rod, so I shouted to him that I was going to wash off the boiler front and footplate, and check both injectors. A Fireman always checks where his mate is before using injectors to avoid a blast in the face with boiling water. Both injectors were working, so I shut off the left hand one, then found my little bit of copper pipe. Most Firemen had this small bit of quarter-inch pipe, slightly flattened at the end, and pushed up into the coal watering pipe, so that cleaning off the footplate and boiler front could be done with high pressure. We were now ready to fill up with water, wash our hands, and go up to the Shed signal on time.

I called up Didcot East Junction ground frame on the telephone and informed them that we were the Southampton standing at the Shed signal. They in turn passed it on to the signal box, so that before I had time to get back on the footplate I could hear the points being set; then as I mounted the last footstep, the signal came off with a bang.

This was a busy time at East Junction Box, and to get us from the Shed signal to the Newbury branch meant a movement of 118 levers, so Fred opened out *River Plym*, and we clattered smartly through the crossovers, over the up relief, down relief, up main, down main, and onto the branch. He gave 'crow' on the whistle to let East Junction know we were over the points, then the road was changed to let us drop gently back onto our train in No. 1 east bay.

Fred buffered up to the first coach, put the brake on and then came down onto the platform to see how I was getting on in coupling up. I managed that like an expert, having no trouble with the vacuum or steam pipes, so much so that he complimented me. What he didn't know was that on the way home after the interview with Bill Young the afternoon before, I had run into Harry Lane the passenger shunter, and on the promise of a couple of pints in the "Prince of Wales" I received half an hour of very instructive tuition on the art of tying a steam engine to a coach!

Our guard was the one and only Walter Beard, the most senior of Western men at Didcot, immaculately turned out as usual, with his white winged collar, black bow tie, and flower in his button hole. He expressed surprise and pleasure on seeing me, saying how it seemed only yesterday that I was a schoolboy. Thus we had on the train that morning a very senior Driver and Guard, and neatly in the middle, a right 'sprog' of a Fireman.

The load was five coaches and two horse boxes, a total of 215 tons — not much compared to the 400-odd the 'Kings' pulled away with, but with 38 stops and starts there and back, the 114 miles over the switchback gradients of the Didcot, Newbury, Winchester, Southampton Branch would mean a wet shirt and a few tons of coal moved.

River Plym was all ready to go; the fire was burning through well, I had a glass full of water in the boiler, and pressure was just on the point of blowing off at the safety valve at 200lbs.

Walter Beard consulted his pocket watch, blew his whistle, waved his green flag, and we were away, collecting the single line token at East Junction for the Upton section.

This was before the building of the double line between Didcot and Newbury, so there would be a lot of tokens to exchange. Fred was in no hurry until we passed over the bridge near the milk depot, then he gave her a bit more on the regulator and began to link her up, but not too much as the climb was 1 in 103. I now began to work in the Western manner; the fire box flaps had been removed because of blackout regulations, so each movement meant opening the fire hole doors. It was a case of open doors, shovel in coal, swing round, coal into fire box, close doors. Although a complicated method to describe it could be carried out with a sweetness that had to be seen.

25

As Fred shut the regulator to run into Upton, I eased on the blower to stop any blow-back and put on the right hand injector, and we came to a stop level with the end of the platform. I now found I had experienced something new in locomotive running, and that was the smell of hot brake blocks. It was an acrid smell and one that I was to become used to over the years, but after shunting jobs it was a surprise that blocks become so hot.

We exchanged tokens with the Signalman for the Compton section, Walter blew his whistle and we were off again up the long drag to the top of the Berkshire Downs at Churn, and it was up this bank and on the sweep down into Compton that a characteristic of the 'Bulldog' Class endeared them to me. At Didcot we had 3376 *River Plym,* 3408 *Bombay,* 3448 *Kingfisher,* and 3407 *Madras,* and they were all very free steamers, but up the banks they had a galloping stride, with the side rods going round in such an easy manner that when they came to a level bit of road or a slight fall, such as we came to through Churn, they literally flew, riding as steady as a coach.

I was beginning to enjoy myself, but on the pull up from Hampstead Norris to Hermitage steam pressure began to drop. The water level dropped also, but Fred was not worried as we had the long drop down into Newbury with the regulator shut and plenty of time to fill the boiler. He knew what had gone wrong, but kept quiet so that I should learn a valuable lesson. I had been a bit over enthusiastic with the shovel and had 'blacked' the fire in; it was a solid mass up to the brick arch.

We ran into Newbury on time, then after the passengers had gone and the station work was completed we pulled up over the main line points, and backed into the bay to wait for a connection.

I got the pricker down and gave the fire a good pull through until it was thick and level all over the box, then as we departed for the Winchester branch, Fred gave *River Plym* half regulator with 35% cut off to Enborne Junction, where we collected the token for Woodhay.

I did not touch the fire, but had a look in the firebox when we ran into the station. It was one great incandescent mass, the steam pressure had come round to the point where she was blowing her head off with the injectors on, and I had so much steam I didn't know what to do with it. I had learnt another lesson; all that work further back down the line just to make steam to blow out of the safety valve! From then on I kept the back-end of the firebox

A photograph of myself on locomotive No. 2222 at Compton in 1945.

Myself by the side of locomotive No. 8400, Stanier Class 8F. Seen here at
Morton Goods loop in 1944.

The U.S.A. Transportation 2-8-0 freight locomotive of Chapter 4. The author sits comfortably in his armchair as Ralph Painton cases her over the junction from Reading West Curve across the Down Main to the Down Relief line. The big Yanks were wonderful engines, except for that very large sand box behind the chimney.

No. 2282 southbound, crosses with the local goods at Upton Station on the Didcot, Newbury, Winchester Branch in single line days. The 22xx class were used almost exclusively on the branch and were complete masters of all traffic requirements.

Churchward's 28xx Class as discussed in Chapter 5 and 7. I must have fired every 28xx on the Great Western, they were the finest heavy goods engines in the country. No. 2847 illustrated is in beautiful condition. Note crosshead vacuum pump under footstep on the framing, front screw coupling hung on buffer beam, (the mark of a good fireman), and the position of the reversing lever; the guides shows she is linked up to about 45% cut off. Not a wisp of steam leaks to be seen, the slight water leaking from the waste pipe under the footsteps would indicate that the right hand live steam injector is in use.

Bert Edmunds and Vic Smith at Paddington, all ready to leave with No. 5069 *Isambard Kingdom Brunel* on the 6.45pm. Both wear a large hankerchief round their necks to combat the coal dust. Vic wears the badge of honour for a Fireman on 'The Runners' — a black beret. As a bare handed Fireman myself I would suggest the gloves would indicate that Vic was courting!

A beautiful photograph of Jackie Wilkins in the early days when my father was a young Fireman lodging with him. Jack is a member of the group of Didcot enginemen shown in the group illustration. He was a grand old gentleman in the days of one Driver, one Engine. Photograph taken around the 1920's.

Bert Edmonds prepares No. 5069 *Isambard Kingdom Brunel* in Old Oak Common shed. Note the blast of smoke from the chimney, Vic Smith has the blower well and truly hard on as he raises steam for the run. *Kenneth Leech*

Driver Potter and Fireman Peedle at high speed on 'The Bristolian'. *Kenneth Leech*

BACK ROW STANDING
1. P. BROWN
2. F. ESSEX
3. G. JONES
4. J. WILKINS
5. A. WAITE
6. J. TALBOT
7. W. GASSON
8. T. BROWN
9. T. POWELL
10. J. PAXTON
11. F. WILLETTS
12. W. SANDELL
13. A. BUSBY
14. E. NOBES
15. H. RYMAN
16. H. HARRIS
17. W. PRIOR
18. W. CHAUNDY

2nd ROW STANDING
19. F. WHEELER
20. J. WIGLEY
21. A. HITCHCOCK
22. I. ROLF
23. P. STROUD
24. C. MINTY
25. A. DURGESS
26. R. BROTHERTON
27. H. GASSON
28. F. ALLAN
29. W. COBB
30. E. CARTER
31. C. BENFIELD
32. T. BAILEY
33. T. PEEDLE
34. R. BECK
35. J. KING
36. F. JONES
37. F. HOLT
38. C. POWELL

2nd ROW SEATED
39. P. HALLPORT
40. J. NICHOLLS
41. T. GRAINGER
42. J. WILEY
43. J. HENDERSON
44. R. CLARKE
45. G. BOWERING
46. R. SAUNDERS
47. E. EDMONDS
48. S. FREEMAN
49. W. JONES
50. S. BATEMAN
51. J. BECKENHAM
52. H. HOLMES
53. J. WILKINS
54. H. CUDMORE

1st ROW SEATED
55. J. HERMOND
56. H. WALKER
57. R. ACKERS
58. A. BOWERING
59. L. PULLIN
60. R. FREWING
61. L. TUGWELL
62. M. WIGLEY
63. R. HAYCROFTE
64. A. COOK
65. W. FREWIN
66. A. CLARGO
67. P. WEST

The Didcot Locomotive Drivers and Firemen outside the "Prince of Wales" during the 1926 ASLEFF strike.

No. 2937 *Clevedon Court* stands at the head of an up express at Birmingham Snow Hill, February 20, 1939. This engine was station pilot at Reading one day in 1938 when a "King," working the down "Bristolian" high speed express broke down. Despite several checks *Clevedon Court* improved on the exacting schedule and ran the 82 miles to Bristol at an average speed of 72mph.

N. Shepherd

A fine illustration of Driver Potter in action on the footplate. One hand rests on the reverser ready to knock down the clip, the other gently rests on the vacuum brake handle. Note speed restriction book and pocket book in the cab tray above his head.   *Kenneth Leech*

Fireman Jack Peedle gives the photographer a cheery wave from the cab of 'The Bristolian'.   *Kenneth Leech*

The Royal Pair again on No. 4056 *Princess Margaret*. She was just out of Swindon shops when this photograph was taken and she was in the usual Swindon immaculate condition.

Kenneth Leech

The great Bert Potter himself. He is typical of the 'Top Link' driver; the gentle smile radiates complete confidence from a gentleman who is a Master craftsman.

Kenneth Leech

Bert Edmonds and Vic Smith at Chippenham with No. 4089 *Donnington Castle* on the 8.20 a.m. Weston-super-Mare to Paddington. *Kenneth Leech*

Albert Potter and Jack Peedle on the same train with No. 4056 *Princess Margaret* at Chippenham a week later. *Kenneth Leech*

Bert Edmonds and Vic Smith push 'The Bristolian' along at 100mph. Home to Mother is a great incentive to get a move on.
Kenneth Leech

Albert Potter and Jack Peedle with No. 5048 *Earl of Devon*. The locomotive is in beautiful condition, but soon to rust away in a scrap yard, her footplate to become fertile ground for grass and chickweed, and her polished brass and copper stripped off for the melting pot.
Kenneth Leech

B.R. 32600/28

BRITISH TRANSPORT COMMISSION

W. N. PELLOW, M.I.Mech.E.
Motive Power Supt.

H. G. KERRY, M.I.Mech.E.
Asst. Motive Power Supt.　M.

Telephone
SWINDON 2611

Ext.　2383

Telegraphic Address
POWER RAILWAY SWINDON

MOTIVE POWER
SUPERINTENDENT
WESTERN REGION
SWINDON, WILTS

Our Reference R.3438

Your Reference 1.

Monday, 28th March, 1955.

Dear Peedell,

   I am pleased to inform
you that the train working arrangements
in connection with the recent journey
of Her Majesty The Queen on Saturday,
March 26th, was very satisfactory so
far as this Department is concerned.

   To mark the occasion of
your having worked the train conveying
Her Majesty The Queen from Shrewsbury
to Windsor, I have pleasure in
enclosing a gratuity of 10s. Od.
in recognition, and to thank you for
the services you so ably rendered on
this occasion.

   Yours truly,

Fireman J.A. Peedell,
Old Oak Common.

One example of many letters from Management to Jack Peedle for his Royal Train working.
The Driver would receive a similar letter, but his gratuity would be 20s.0d!

An inside shot of my first signal box at Milton, after my transfer from the Loco. Department. This Box was to be the start of another career as exacting in it's way as the footplate. It was one box that was never short of coal, even if some of my mates considered I had deserted them. Note tomato plants between levers, each job has it's perks!

packed tight and let the fire slope gently down to the front end. Fred never said a word, bless him; he knew the value of learning by mistakes. We arrived at Winchester dead on time, sliding out of the tunnel so quietly that we caught the station staff on the hop.

We left Winchester over the long 40ft high Shawford viaduct to Shawford Junction, to join the old London and South Western Railway, by now the Southern, and ran down into Eastleigh where we were booked for ten minutes. Fred and I gazed at the many strange locomotives, and I saw both the most horrible locomotive and one of the most beautiful engines that morning.

Up the main line towards us came one of Mr. Bulleid's indescribable 'Q' Class. Later I had a chance to go aboard one and came away most impressed.

Leaving Eastleigh Fred set the regulator just off the jockey valve so that we would drift past a place he knew I would want to see just at the end of the platform—Eastleigh Works and Shed. It covered a large area reminiscent of Swindon, with sidings full of engines of every shape and age, and I remember that I fervently wished I could have a look round it all, but that time was in the future, I was later to get to know Eastleigh Shed very well.

At the Shed signal, waiting to come out, was one of the most beautiful steam locomotives I had ever seen—a compliment, indeed, for a Great Western man to make, but it was deserved. She was so graceful, her green paint work had a deep transcendent lustre, proof of much loving care; her side rods sparkled in the sunshine and looked so delicate that they reminded me of photographs I had seen of *La France;* even the copper pipes from the cylinder drain cocks had been burnished. She was 2333 *Remembrance.* I wrote the name and number down, determined to find out more about her at the first opportunity.

When we arrived at Southampton Terminus I uncoupled, and the coaches were drawn back by the station passenger pilot engine. We followed the train as far as the platform edge while the train carried on clear of the points. The road was set to allow us onto the turn-table, then while we turned *River Plym* our train was propelled back into the station, where the pilot engine came off. We were all ready to start the long haul back.

I coupled up again, then got up on the tender and brought the coal forward, while Fred went round oiling the bars and glands. This completed, we had our sandwiches, a drink out of the tea bottles, and then Fred settled down to make his log ticket up to date, for we had twenty minutes to spare. I told Fred that I was going over to the Southern pilot engine for a few minutes, as I wanted to know a lot more about the engine we had seen at Eastleigh.

I asked permission to climb up on the footplate of the T9 and was made most welcome by the driver and fireman. Both were middle-aged, and seemed surprised by my youth. When I mentioned that beautiful engine I found I was in the company of two gentlemen who knew all about her. I was told that she was a former London, Brighton, and South Coast Railway engine; she was one of four locomotives designed and built as 4—6—4 express passenger tanks by Mr. Billington for the LBSC Railway, and later re-built as tender engines. The one I had seen at the Shed signal at Eastleigh was named *Remembrance* in memory of the railway lads who had died in the Great War.

Both the Southern men were very enthusiastic about these engines, and appreciated the fact that I was so interested in them. The Fireman said that they were free-steaming if fired all over the box, and that they would run like the wind.

This bit of information was to come in handy in 1942, because 2330 *Cudworth,* 2331 *Beattie,* 2332 *Stroudley,* and 2333 *Remembrance* were transferred on loan to the Great Western to help out an engine shortage, together with three of Mr. Urie's Moguls 496, 498, and 499. We all had a bit of a surprise when we did get our hands on them; to our chagrin we found that the Southern engines were very good.

At 11.30am we began the long drag back home. From Southampton to just the other side of Burghclere it was a steady climb. We stopped and started so many times I began to wonder if we should ever see Didcot again.

One interesting incident came our way as we were between Eastleigh and Shawford Junction, where we saw the first of Mr. Bullied's "Merchant Navy" Class Pacifics, *Channel Packet,* tearing down towards us. We had heard rumours of this locomotive which could show our "Kings" a thing or two, but she went flashing by at such a speed she was just a blur of slab-sided metal, with no exhaust audible but just the roar of the coaches. From Fred's side I looked back along our train to see her last coaches swaying and rapidly diminishing in the distance. We were both very impressed.

We plugged away on towards home until Compton was reached. There I pushed the fire all over the box, splashed a bit round her, and put the shovel down for the last time; it was downhill now, and with *River Plym* going to Shed there was enough in the firebox to see her through.

I swept up the footplate, then sat down on the tip-up seat. A feeling of utter exhaustion came over me, my back and legs ached, the palm of my right hand was sore and bruised from the hundreds of times I had hit up the live steam injector handle. I was a very tired sixteen year old boy. The glamour had gone, and I just wanted to curl-up and rest.

The chatter from the chimney softened as Fred linked her up, then I felt his hand on my shoulder. He pointed out a hare running level with us in a field; he gave me a squeeze and said I would be better tomorrow, as I would know the road and engine, and that the first time was always the worst. He was pleased with the way I had handled the job and said he would tell Bill Young so, and that he would insist that I remained with him all the week. With a wink he said I had not let the fire out once.

It was the encouragement I needed. I looked over the side and watched that side rod go round and round with the regularity of a clock and felt a great satisfaction in knowing it was my efforts which had made it possible. At a rough guess I had shovelled 3½ tons of coal, and boiled away over 3,500 gallons of water to keep that side rod moving. I placed a pad of cotton waste in my hand and hit up the injector handle for the last time as Fred shut off to run into Didcot east bay. I felt a lot better.

Relief was waiting for us when we stopped. As we walked down the platform towards the Shed to book off, the solid surface of the platform seemed strange after the movement of the last few hours. I looked back towards *River Plym* with affection; she had responded to an amateur perfectly, and I would never forget her.

The next few day were as Fred had predicted. Things were a lot better, for I could anticipate him shutting off for station stops, I had a 'feel' for the engine working, and could sit down at intervals of easy running. I was beginning to get to know the Didcot, Newbury, and Winchester Branch; in fact the time was to come when I knew every rail-joint, bridge, bank, and person, throughout the whole length of the line. It saddens me now, when on a fine summer Sunday I have a run down to Southsea in the car and see the broken bridges, deserted signal boxes, and the air of desolation over the miles of ballast, empty of rails. To me and all the old Didcot steam enginemen, it is a loss keenly felt.

Saturday came, and with it my last trip over the Branch for some time, for when I eventually did become a Fireman there were the pilot and goods links to go through first, with only the occasional passenger job to cover.

This last day also brought a change of engines. We were given another 'Bulldog", 3448 *Kingfisher*, because *River Plym* was due for a boiler washout. I felt a little peeved about this as I had come to regard her as my regular engine, and could now understand the feelings of enginemen who had their own engines in the old days. I had a look round the Shed for her, and found her at the bottom of No. 4 road standing 'dead'.

I climbed up on footplate and could feel the coldness about her. It was an alien atmosphere, devoid of the warmth and life of the previous days; her footplate was covered with coal, clinker and ash from where her fire had been dropped, she reminded me of a very old lady caught with her teeth out. I felt like a stranger, she had abandoned me. I searched round for her shovel and found it under the fire irons in the rack on the tender. I had become attached to that shovel so I swopped it for the one off *Kingfisher*.

Kingfisher, if anything, was a better locomotive than *River Plym;* her steaming was about the same, and although the exhaust had a crisper bark she did not burn as much coal. This was due to the work of Bill Miles the Foreman Fitter. He had just released *Kingfisher* from his lifting shop and he had set the valves to perfection, and the results of his labours were evident in the way she lifted the train up the banks.

I had time to admire the scenery on that lovely early spring morning; the green of the Downs, the gentle rolling countryside, and the swoop down the bank between Highclere and Burghclere.

I always enjoyed that little bit of the Winchester Branch. Leaving Highclere the road dropped to 1 in 106 bank into Burghclere. We would tear down the bank, shoot through the bridge and up the other side like riding a roller coaster at the fair.

Two other places to enjoy were the drop down from Litchfield into Whitchurch, with the town stretched out on our left hand side looking like a model township in the morning sunshine; and crossing the 2,000-odd feet of the 40ft high Shawford viaduct across the valley from St. Catherine's Hill down to Shawford Junction.

The other side of the picture was, of course, the punch back up again on the return journey; but who cared, on a sunny day with the engine steaming well, good Welsh coal in the tender, and a Driver who had not only a gentleman but a Great Western engineman who had a complete understanding of his engine and of his young Fireman.

Thank you Fred Essex, you were a great man to know, and I look back with nostalgic memories of those happy days with you on *River Plym* and *Kingfisher*.

The next week I was back to earth with a bump, on nights coaling engines, and sure enough it was blowing a gale from the north straight into the coal stage, so that every tub of coal tipped into the tender waiting below sent up a cloud of dust. Within an hour I was as black as any miner who had dug that coal out. A shovel and 20 tons of coal from a common bond between miners and steam locomotive Firemen.

Between the odd jobs of coaling, fire dropping, ash loading, and all the other dirty, filthy jobs connected with the turn-round of steam engines, I had the firing turns cropping up more frequently on the many yard pilots and Didcot depot pilots, so in turn I fired for every Driver at Didcot. Some of the older men were a bit grouchy—and so I expect I should be if I were nearly 65 years old and had to get out of bed at 4.30 in the morning—but on the whole they were not a bad lot.

The younger Drivers would let me have a go on the regulator and I soon became skilled in shunting a load of 70 wagons with a pannier tank engine, all good training for enginemanship.

The months crept on until the last weekend of August, and on my birthday, August 28th, I was notified that I had been appointed Fireman at Didcot; my Registered Number for seniority was 27297. I was at last a Great Western Steam Locomotive Fireman.

Big Harold and I went home to Charcotte that weekend where I had great satisfaction in informing Grandfather Gasson that I was a professional now.

3

Firing Days

I booked on duty that first day as a Fireman at 5.45am with a sense of pride, and looking back on it now I still feel proud that the Great Western considered me competent enough to entrust me with their locomotive boilers. I had now come up from junior Cleaner to junior Fireman, a system that ran to junior Fireman in the relief link, number three link, number two link, to the passenger link; then, good fortune prevailing, one became a Driver, junior of course, and started the whole process again.

Now it was my turn to catch out the junior Cleaner with requests that he go to the stores for a tin of vacuum dust to rub on the brake blocks, and a key for the smoke-box door, or for good measure to see if they had in stock a left handed shovel or coal pick. We all fell for it in our turn, but it was good clean fun.

One thing I could never understand was the system of priorities applicable to all enginemen, whether they be G.W.R., L.N.E.R., L.M.S. or Southern, compared to other occupations. In a young man's world you have pilots, racing car drivers, speedway and racing motorcyclists, all with the reactions and state of mind that goes with youth, yet the average express passenger driver was a solid man in his early sixties, undoubtedly a grandfather, who would get out of a warm bed, cycle a couple of miles to the Shed, light a smoking dirty old flare lamp, and crawl about in a pit oiling a great steam locomotive. He would make a thorough job of preparation, back it on to a train of coaches with a dead weight of 400 tons, then proceed to nurse it, coax it, love it, and sometimes swear at it, but with all the aplomb of the youths listed above he would then go tearing off at 90 to 100 miles an hour; the top link man in steam days was without doubt a special breed of man.

It was to be some months before I had a regular Driver, as I was one of several 'spare' Firemen to be found in every Shed, a dogsbody to be at the whim of the shift Foreman's command, which usually meant engine preparation which was a thankless task when all the work was for another Fireman, and after the fourth engine one began to feel a sense of injustice; but all loco men had it in their turn so it was not so bad as it felt at the time.

Mr. Mathews, the Chief Clerk, would write out the duty list in his beautiful copperplate handwriting and place it in the glass panels in the booking-on hall where I would sometimes find my name on it as a Fireman to one of the shunting turns. It would list the time of booking on, time off shed, engine number, Driver and Fireman's name, and the duty, e.g. up yard pilot, or Moreton yard pilot), but usually I would find I had been booked 'as required' or 'shed assisting'. Both jobs were about the same, but Mr. Mathews had a great sense of humour, he thought I would like a change now and again! He was a very tall, gaunt man who came to work on a large double-framed bicycle of great antiquity; he also wore a trilby hat and raincoat that were equal in age.

The very large wicker basket on the handle-bars contained his paper and lunch; if ever there was a 'ringer' for a retired Bishop then Mr. Mathews was that, he could have made a fortune in the film industry. But looks are deceptive; Mr. Young might be the Shed Foreman in charge, but Mr. Mathews ran it, he was very much the Chief Clerk with all the authority the Great Western gave to such a position, but he was always a gentleman in every sense of the word.

The duty 'shed assisting' had its lighter moments, as this enabled one to do the odd spot of driving, helping the Shed Driver to turn and stable locomotives, but it also had its hazards.

Moving engines after they had the fire cleaned and had been coaled meant they were short of steam—the most one could expect was 80lbs in the boiler—so judgement of stopping distance and careful control of the hand brake had some hairy moments. Even so, I can remember only one incident that was a disaster, although it was a laugh at the time.

We had on loan from the L.N.E.R. some of the old Great Central Robinson's R.O.D. engines, still in original condition, and like the engines of this class the Great Western had bought, horrible lumps of machinery. The original engines had the horizontal regulator which was pulled towards one, but they had a fault which I expect the North Eastern men were fully aware of, but which the Great Western men did not find on a Swindon boiler; if the water in the gauge glass was over three-quarters full you could open the regulator all right but you could not shut it again, which of course led to complications when it came to stopping.

Standing first under the coal stage ready to be turned was one of these R.O.D. engines, L.N.E.R. No. 6265.

Four of us clambered up on her footplate to take her down to the turn-table and then place her in the 'field' as we termed Nos. 7 and 8 roads. She had a glass full of white water, indicating the need of a long overdue boiler washout, and 80lbs showing on the steam gauge, just enough steam to complete the movement.

Once on the footplate we found it rather restricted, as both sides of the cab were built up with two raised wooden platforms, leaving a narrow well for the Fireman to work in, so we could see that care would have to be taken when swinging a shovel to avoid tearing skin from one's knuckles. The fireman elected to driver her was a diminutive little Welsh lad, so he stood up on the raised platform and gave the regulator a tentative pull towards him but nothing happened; then he placed one foot up against the boiler casing and pulled hard with both hands.

The old R.O.D. gave a lurch and slipped with a roar, sending up a great column of dirty water from her chimney as she primed, showering the whole area with fine wet soot, but the regulator would not close completely. There was a sound from the regulator valve like a fish frier, and at walking pace she began to move with a clank, clank from each side rod as it came round, and with the regularity of a pile-driver.

With the weariness of an old lady she clanked her way towards the turn-table. I rode on the bottom step and dropped off near the lifting shop to change the point for the engine already on the table, expecting to hear the soft beat of the exhaust stop as the regulator was shut. Instead I saw two of my mates jump off her with some urgency and saw her remorselessly clank on to the inevitable end.

The turn-table was half-way round with a Collet 0—6—0 2226 on it when the old lady reached the end of the rails. Both Driver and Fireman of 2226 had a look of utter disbelief on their faces as that old R.O.D. dropped over the well of the table and buried her nose in the ballast.

She stopped then, all right, shearing off both front cylinder cocks which clouded her in steam and emptied the boiler in the process.

We forgot the seriousness of the situation and burst out laughing, for she looked so ridiculous sitting there with her nose in the ground, cab tilted up over the tender, but bad news travels with the speed of light in a locomotive Shed and within minutes the whole Shed staff were gathered round, with Bill Young making noises that all Shed Foremen make when things go wrong.

There was plenty of advice on how to get her out, some of it good, some of it a bit hairbrained, but all well intended and all of which Bill Miles ignored—a Foreman Fitter has his own ideas on how to tackle such a situation, and as soon as the dust had settled he gathered his lads together with blocks and jacks and set about getting her out.

The turn-table was out of action for the rest of the day, so all engines that had to be turned were coupled together and sent off shed to turn via West Curve and Foxhall Junction.

Orders came out reminding us of the rule book that in future only Passed Firemen and Drivers were to move engines, but it only lasted a few weeks. The War was on and every engine had to be serviced and back on the road as soon as was possible, so it was a question of all hands mucking in, and as long as incidents such as the one just related were few and far between then the job got done.

The R.O.D. engine and the Western counterpart were not engines that were loved. Along with Webb's 26XX Class, the 'Aberdares', and Mr. Riddle's 2–8–0 'Austerity' Class, we referred to them as members of the bovine species, except that they did not give milk!

The R.O.D. and the Aberdares were fine engines in their day but by the time my generation of Firemen laid hands on them they were long past their best. The Austerity Class did some good work, they were without frills, and easy to maintain, but as every Great Western engineman knew, Mr. Riddles need not have gone to all that trouble to design and build them; all that he needed was a set of drawings from Swindon of the 28XX Class, for they could do all that was required for freight working, Mr. Churchward had seen to that in 1903.

Later on honour was satisfied to some extent when the War Office sanctioned the building of Sir William Stanier's Class 8F for the L.M.S. The Swindon-built engines started at 84XX and as the designer had worked for many years at Swindon with Mr. Churchward we found we had a part-Great Western Engine after all.

A lot of Swindon was built into them and they proved to be fine locomotives with plenty of room in a comfortable cab. Unfortunately, the injector handles were large heavy brass wheels with a spoke sticking out of the side, designed to make a whacking great blister in the palm of one's hand. When they were shut off the spindle would expand so that the adjustable spanner was always to be found on the tray over the fire-hole door, and at the last resort the coal pick was brought into use. I could never understand why the Great Western injector handle was never made standard on these engines; this was made of wood on a steel spindle, it was cheap to produce and easily replaceable, particularly as brass was at a premium in those days.

At this period of time our main preoccupation was the lack of tools. It was a nightmare to prepare engines, as overnight coal-picks, headlamps, gauge-lamps, hand brushes, shovels and even deflector shields disappeared. It got so bad that we made up the fire as best we could with our bare hands then went searching the other engines on shed to rob them of their tools. It deteriorated to such an extent that the only way to obtain the items needed to go off shed was to go back up the ash road and meet engines as they came in for service. At one period when we had the same engine all the week and took her off shed and returned with her, my Mate and I would tie all the tools with strong twine and lower them into the tank of the tender, making sure we had allowed the water level to drop well down! It was demoralising to see Drivers and Firemen creeping about in pits, either looking for tools or hiding them to use the next day; we were being turned into a band of scroungers and thieves. Morale was at a very low point when this came on top of long hours on duty with bad coal and engines in urgent need of repair, but we carried on and made the best of it; we were still Great Western and proud of it.

At the end of October I was teamed up at last with a regular Driver in the pilot link, and I was in luck.

The first Driver a young Fireman has as a Mate can make a profound impression on him, and my time with Ben Foxwell was a happy one. Ben was one of three ex-Cardiff main line men I was fortunate enough to have as Mates and from each one I was to learn something valuable. I don't think it was possible to upset Ben, he was a very quiet man, kind and considerate, completely unruffled under any set of circumstances that came along.

I was inclined to get a bit agitated when the engine would not steam as it should, but Ben would look in the firebox, offer some good advice, and all would be well again. From him I learned to have confidence in myself and the need for patience. I know that he was worried about his family enduring the bombing of Cardiff, and for his sake I was hopeful that his application to return to his home shed would be soon, but he freely gave his help to me when I needed it most.

The greater part of my time with Ben was shunting Moreton

Yard. This had just been built but no water supply had been connected, so we were given tender engines to shunt the many trains that called there, but what engines they were. They were little old L.M.S. 0—6—0's of 1885 vintage, (the numbers I have in my diary are 3103, 3485, and 3196) about the same size as a Dean Goods Engine; but there any resemblance ended, for they couldn't pull the skin off a rice pudding. I have read that pre-war the L.M.S. enginemen ran passenger trains with them, but the thought of it makes me shudder, those engines were an abomination.

There was a set procedure to go through when attempting to re-marshal a train from the goods loop. We would couple onto the first wagon with a full boiler and a full head of steam, then back away up the spur towards the bridge to clear the yard points, but this was done with a great deal of slipping, panting and groaning that was torture to hear, and by the time we had cleared the points we had no steam or water, so we had a 'blow up' before starting to shunt. This called for fog working, because the spindle glands were leaking so badly that once the regulator was opened the whole front of the engine was enveloped in steam, and the shunter could not be seen!

It was in such un-dignified circumstances that Ben's old Driver found us one day. He came tearing along the up main line on a South Wales express, blasting away on the whistle and making gestures, half hanging out of the cab of his 'Castle' to attract our attention. He got in return the shrill blast of an L.M.S. whistle and the victory sign, but not in the way Mr. Churchill meant it. From then on, every up or down South Wales express went through the same performance and received the same reply. As I have said earlier, on a family railway such as the Great Western news travels very fast indeed, and to see Ben, an ex-main line man, messing about on a worn-out old Midland engine was too good to be true. The news went round Cardiff Shed with almost the speed of light.

They were a good lot though. Cigarettes were hard to obtain in the Didcot area, but the Cardiff men would throw a packet of twenty out of the cab and always with a message of good cheer wrapped round the packet. It did Ben good; he did not feel so far from home, but he did look a bit wistful at the last coach disappearing in the distance.

In the New Year of 1942 the water was connected up to the water columns at Moreton and we lost the little L.M.S. engines to the local pick-up jobs. We now had the proper tools for the job, our 57XX and 36XX pannier tanks. Those engines would lift a load

37

of 60 twenty-tonners out of the up goods loop with an angry aggressiveness that was a joy to see. Moreton Yard proved to be such a success that it was extended out into a cornfield, but with the second yard the cutting was not dug out; instead it was graded to make a hump yard. We had three pannier tank engines working hard 24 hours each day by the end of 1943.

1942, however, saw a small revolution in the habits of footplate staff—it was the year of the Tea Can.

Because of the lack of canteen facilities we were allowed a small ration of tea and sugar. The firebox brew-up was born and the pint whisky bottles were thrown away; no more cold tea. With this revolution was also born a very enterprising business. It was possible to buy commercially made tea cans holding a pint, but two cups each are not enough for thirsty loco men. However loco boilersmiths could make and supply two-pint cans.

These cans were made of heavy-gauge tinplate and were a joy to behold, the soldering was sheer artistry while the base was a good solid one; the lads who made the oil cans could certainly turn their hands to other things, they knew the requirements of the customer, and at 3/6d a time those tea cans were value for money.

There were three main supply points in the area, the boilersmith's shops at Old Oak Common, Banbury, and Wolverhampton, and you placed your order with whoever you were relieving on the road at that time, but it was recognised that the Wolverhampton-manufactured can had the edge on the other makers and was worth waiting for.

Once acquired the can was cherished and protected with all the love given to a young wife. It was a symbol of cheer in those dreary days, and to be offered a cup of tea out of another man's can was a mark of comradeship. The art of making the tea was a performance equal to anything seen in the kitchen. The first movement was to protect the can, and this was done by plastering the bottom and sides up to the water line with thick oil, then it was placed on the fire using the handle of the coal pick through the handle of the can.

On big engines the fire was built up over the firebox ring in true Great Western fashion, so a little platform was dug out and the can placed on the red hot coals. By the time one had got the tea out of the food-box the water was boiling; the can was then lifted out and the tea thrown on top, the lid placed on, and then put on the firebox tray where the oil was wiped off. The result was a perfect cup of tea.

One thing we did learn quickly was to keep the lid on. It was known to get eight cups of a six-cup can, particularly at night, and this phenomenon could always be traced to a leaking regulator valve! We would eat a cheese sandwich in the dark with a perfect finger and thumb print in the corner of the bread quite cheerfully, but tea topped up from a dirty boiler was another matter.

The main requirement was, of course, clean fresh water, but at a push we would use boiler water if we had nothing else. The second requirement was knowledge of the road. It was a regular manoeuvre on a long run—regulator shut, can in, then two minutes of coasting and out with the can. The right measure of tea went in and the regulator was opened again with only a slight drop in running time.

On a passenger train, if the guard noticed a momentary pause he would book 'signal check', the passenger might think 'one in front', but to the two men on the engine doing all the work it was our tea break.

It was quite a work of art to pour out a drink when on a fast-running train without spilling any, but we became experts. There was always the regular spot when we knew it was possible for the brew-up; my favourite place was on the Berks and Hants Line going down. My Mate would shut off as we cleared the top of Savernake Bank, then it was downhill all the way to Westbury, with plenty of time to enjoy a drink and clear it all away before Heywood Road Junction signals came into view.

One thing we had to come to a clear understanding on, was the drink we were going to have. We had stopped for signals on a dirty wet night and on this occasion my Mate decided he would like a cup of Oxo for a change—very nice so long as he had told me of this important change in plans.

I placed the can on the fire and as soon as it reached boiling point I turned round to get the tea, but while I was engaged in this my Mate had lifted the can out and put in two Oxo cubes. The tea went on top, was given a stir and then placed on the firebox tray to brew.

It was after the second cup that my Mate made a remark about his Oxo tasting queer, and I said the tea tasted a bit off, but we got the rest of it down. A couple of hours later we both made a quick dash to the toilets!

Some members of the traffic department had what is known as "fringe benefits" coming with the introduction of the tea can; these members were the signalmen. There was no contract between locomotivemen and signalmen but by mutual agreement a fair rate of exchange was soon arrived at—one can of boiling water from the signal box kettle was equal to half a ton of coal in the signal-box bunker.

Rule 55, which requires the Fireman to go to the signal box to remind the signalman of the presence of the train at his signals, was carried out with a regularity that would gladden the heart of any Inspector. There were no cold signalmen or thirsty footplate men, and it was an agreement that lasted until the end of steam. When the last steam engine ran on British Railways the tears in the eyes of signalmen were not just nostalgic ones.

At the end of Febuary I was working my last week with Ben. A new link had been formed to relieve the many goods trains now running and I was to go up into this link, so I would be on the main line at last.

Ben read a bit in the newspaper that still makes me chuckle when I think back on it. The Ministry of Food issued a statement that all juveniles up to the age of seventeen years and six months engaged on war work and/or shift work and without the facilities of a canteen were to be allowed hot cocoa between the fourth and fifth hour of work. Ben dared me to try it on Bill Young, so I took him up on it just for a bit of fun.

I made a formal application to see the Shed Foreman on a domestic matter, and at this stage I would not request the presence of my Union representative. I was notified to book on duty half an hour early the next day, when the Foreman would see me.

The next day I knocked on Bill Young's door and walked in. He was sitting behind his desk with a neutral look on his face; poor man, he hadn't a clue as to what it was all about.

I showed him the newspaper cutting which he read, then I asked him what time would it be convenient for him to prepare my hot cocoa. Bill sat there very quiet for several seconds, in fact I can still remember the loud ticking of the clock in his office and the dust dancing in a shaft of sunlight across his desk; it is referred to I think as a 'pregnant pause'. Bill very slowly and carefully tilted his bowler hat further over his right eye, gave it a tap to make quite sure it was on firmly, then he with great deliberation said just two words in Welsh.

Now Welsh is a language I am not conversant with, but I was in no doubt about the two words Bill had spoken; even in Hindustani they would have been understood. I got out before Bill did himself an injury. Ben paid up like a gentleman, I collected twenty Woodbines for that little episode, but kept out of Bill Young's way for a couple of weeks. When I did see him again he gave me a grin and called me a 'cheeky bugger'.

On reflection Bill could see that he had been taken for a gentle leg pulling session and the Gassons had a reputation for this sort of incident, but he did have a couple of pints in the Prince of Wales on the strength of the story.

In the new link I was again Mate to another Cardiff man, Leonard Judd. Len was a short stout man, bubbling over with life. He scorned the engineman's cap for a cloth cap pulled down over his left ear, and from Len I learnt how to fire the big engine. He had been an expert on the main line expresses, and he showed me every trick of the trade. To see him swing a shovel was an exhibition of a master craftsman at work.

Len loved being a Driver, but he had one regret on leaving the ranks of the Firemen, for he had to leave behind his beloved 5020 *Trematon Castle.* This engine was one of the regular engines Len had fired when he was on the 'runners' and according to him there was not another 'Castle' like her, she was perfection, and every engine on which we worked was compared to her—Len never missed the opportunity to relate some story about 5020. We would see her sometimes when we were running on the up relief line between Didcot and Reading. She would come sliding up alongside on the up main line with that beautiful easy gait of a 'Castle' in tip-top condition, with just a wisp of steam coming from her safety valve, her copper cap and paintwork gleaming in the sun. She was a credit to Cardiff Shed.

There would be a shouted conversation between us as she slowly crept by, and if it was Len's ex-driver some good natured advice on how to drive a steam engine would be shouted across the gap between us; then her greater speed would take her on and away.

Apart from the many 'Halls', 'Manors', 'Granges', 43XX, 28XX, and other classes we had a few big engines, 4082 *Windsor Castle,* 4038 *Queen Berengaria,* 4062 *Malmesbury Abbey,* 4045 *Prince John,* to name but a few, and most of the 'Saints' still in service. Each one was compared to *Trematon Castle* with unfavourable remarks from Len.

I shall never forget my first trip on a 'Saint', or a 'Forty'. Those great 6ft.8½in wheels would begin to revolve so slowly when the regulator was opened, then they would start to run like a race horse.

If ever there was an engine to be compared to a lady of breeding then the 'Forties' were that; for the first time I could really appreciate the genius of Mr. Churchward. It was sacrilege to work them on a goods train, which was the only time we had a chance to handle an engine of quality, but to work them back to their home shed was the economic way with the shortage of engines. We looked after them with special care.

Wednesday March 18th was a very special day in the life of Len and myself. We booked on at 10.00am and were given a job straight away, to relieve the 4.30am Avonmouth to Acton standing at Didcot West Box. When we saw the engine I could hardly contain myself. It was 2333 *Remembrance*, the former London, Brighton, and South Coast engine I had seen and admired so much at Eastleigh the year before. Len was pleased for me as I had talked almost as much about her as he had about *Trematon Castle*, and he welcomed the chance to try a Southern express engine.

She was not in the pristine condition of a year ago, but she was still a fine looking locomotive. We climbed aboard and had a look at our unfamiliar surroundings. Everything was recognisable, if in a different place, so we would manage.

There was a Locomotive Inspector with the engine to see how Western men could handle a strange engine, but I cannot remember his name. He was a South Wales man and on first name terms with Len. The Swindon men we relieved were not too impressed with *Remembrance*; the Fireman said she was a bit shy in steaming, and this was confirmed by the Inspector.

When they were gone I had a look in the firebox. The fire was built up in Great Western manner, right up to the firebox ring. The firebox door was a strange contraption—it worked like a baker's oven door, swinging back on a hinge. When in the closed position there was a small flap in the middle that could be lifted up and secured by a ratchet. With a small narrow shovel the Southern men used it would be possible to fire her through this flap, but not with the Great Western shovel, or with the large Welsh steam coal.

I remembered what the Southern fireman had told me the year before about firing all over the box, so I got the long pricker out of the tender rack and pushed the fire about until it was level, then, as she started to lift her safety valve, I had a test run on the injectors. Both picked up at once with a sweet singing, higher pitched than the Western injector but with a clear healthy sound. Len and I were satisfied, we gave a short 'toot' on the whistle and at once the home and distant signal dropped.

We had a load of 48 banana vans all loose-coupled, so as soon as I had unwound the tender handbrake, Len opened the ejector, blew the brakes off and eased open the regulator.

She move forward with a soft 'whoof, whoof' from the chimney, so unlike the crisp bark of the Great Western exhaust, but by the time we were half-way through the station she was beginning to speed up and Len had to wind her up to shorten the valve travel. We had a clear road, which was a change. I left her alone until we were passing Moreton, then I opened the firebox door, leaving it open and started to fire her all over the box. I could smell scorching and could see Len edging away, for with the door open Len's overall trousers were beginning to steam. I had her on the boil all right! Len made sure he was standing well back when he saw me reach for the shovel. He found that the tender running plate was the coolest place.

Remembrance was not shy of steam, the needle stood still on the red line even when the injector was on.

At each signal box we passed the Signalman was looking out of the window to see this great Southern locomotive on Western metals, and each signal box was a sign for the Inspector to make an entry in his pocket book. I had a quick look over his shoulder to see what it was all about and could see a list of passing points and the words 'boiler pressure constant'.

It was a morning to remember, for except for a check through Reading we ran all the way to Acton Yard. Going through Reading, though, we saw a Southern engine at Reading East Main waiting to come out of New Junction. They blasted away on the whistle and waved their caps, and as we returned the compliment *Remembrance* lifted her safety valve with a roar as if to show she was in good hands.

We took her to Old Oak Common Shed from Acton Yard, and placed her on the ash road with regret. Even with the fire run down she still steamed; we were very impressed with a fine locomotive. All three of us walked away from her chatting about some incident on the trip up, and I felt on top of the world. Not only had I had a wonderful morning on a strange engine and had made her steam where others had failed, but a real live Locomotive Inspector was referring to me as 'son'. I felt I had arrived, I was a Main Line Fireman.

Before the year was out I had fired all of her sister engines, each in the same manner, and each one was a good locomotive, but

Remembrance was more than a name to me now. Even Len, with all his affection for *Trematon Castle,* had to admit she was something special.

We had our tea and sandwiches at Old Oak Common, in the engineman's mess room, then reported to the Shift Foreman who, like all Shift Foremen, had a job all lined up for us. Now a Locomotive Shed Foreman is a man of manners; he uses etiquette unless he is dealing with a Cleaner. He does not give a direct order but suggests, and he suggested that we make our way to the carriage sidings where we would find a train of empty coaching stock for Newport. He also suggested that if we had reported to him earlier we could have taken the engine off shed. We both thought he had a point there but to show that we were good chaps at heart, and not the rogues he thought we were, Len informed him that we knew the road right through and he could tell Control no relief was required. There was an ulterior motive to this of course, but we did not want to spoil his day; Newport is but a stone's throw from Cardiff and Len could see a night at home if we used a little finesse.

We set off from the shed before the Foreman could change his mind, for from the look on his face we could tell that he knew something was not all that it could be, and in our obvious haste we took the wrong path between the lines of coaches and had to walk some distance to get to our train.

We had turned the corner of the long line of coaches towards the train which we were to work back when Len stopped so suddenly that I nearly knocked him over. There facing us was a 'Castle', and on the red painted buffer beam was the number 5020. It was his beloved *Trematon Castle.*

For Len at that moment it was Christmas, birthday, holidays all rolled into one; he gave a little jig, put his arms round me and nearly squeezed my ribs in, and half-walked, half-ran towards her. It was a reunion with a very dear friend.

The Old Oak Common driver began to explain what preparation he had carried out for the journey, and I could see that Leonard was assuming an act of extreme nonchalance while underneath he was seething for these two men to leave. He wanted a few minutes to himself before blowing up for the signal. *Trematon Castle* had failed that morning on the up Fishguard with vacuum trouble; the Old Oak fitters had repaired her and as Cardiff wanted her back quickly Control decided to work her back with the empty coaches.

With a South Wales engine working home they had not coaled her. There was no point in transporting coal all the way from the Welsh pits just to take it back again, so all they had done was to clear all the coal from the back plate of the tender to the front, and a right old mixture it was too.

Len climbed down to do the bars and glands, but this was just an excuse to have a look round her, since the Old Oak driver had already oiled her.

I had a look over the side and saw Len wipe her slide bars with cotton waste. It was a caress, contact with a happy past re-established. I climbed down to join him and placed one hand on his shoulder and together we walked slowly round her without speaking; there was no need for words, it was sufficient to drink in the magnificence of this beautiful locomotive.

Our load was a mixed bunch of coaches; we had 14 on ranging from Webb clerestory to Collet 35 tonners so our total weight behind the tender was about 500 tons.

Len and I climbed back on to her footplate. His eyes were moist as he opened the large ejector to blow off her brakes, and the twin needles climbed up the vacuum gauge and stopped level on the train pipe and reservoir at 25lbs. He shut the ejector, the needles dropped to 22lbs and held. She was all right. I blew the gauge glass through to check the water level, nodded to Len, and we were off; he opened the regulator just enough to glide down to the signal. The 'dummy' came off and we eased out on to the down relief, looking back to see the last coach go through the points, then Len gave her half regulator, knocked down the locking handle on the screw reverser and began to slowly wind her back, letting her take her own time and pace. I started to fire her as Len had taught me, while he began to gently tap down the regulator until she was just off the jockey valve. The cut-off was at 25% and she was beginning to move like a turbine running.

There was no need to hurry. As we came in sight of each distant signal it would be at caution, then as Len raised his finger to cancel the A.T.C. warning buzzer the distant would drop and the shrill ring of the bell would sound in the cab as the shoe under the frame rode over the ramp. We were content to amble along at a steady 35mph so as to avoid catching up the signal in front. It was uncanny the way she rode, each rail joint could be heard under the wheels and the gentle 'slap slap' of the vacuum pump on Len's side.

Between Ealing Broadway station and starting signal I opened the left hand water feed and gave her a full turn on the exhaust injector. It picked up at once, the sound synchronising with the exhaust from the chimney, undulating almost as a symphony with the vacuum pump and wheel beats.

Leonard was happy, he sat there with his arms folded, legs crossed and swinging under his seat, singing 'Saspan Fach' but in English for my benefit. Only one thing was missing, and that was his old shovel.

Most of the Firemen on the 'runners' had their own shovels, not because the standard shovel was at fault, but the artiste demanded a special tool for a specialised job, so they would get a fitter to 'breathe' on one. The sides would be ground down from the middle to the facing edge in a taper, then a little ground off the corners. The result was a sharp cutting tool that was balanced to a nicety and that would cut through coal like a knife. Len's shovel had been so doctored, but to compensate for his short reach they had fitted a longer shaft for him. He had said goodbye to that shovel when he was made Driver and posted to Didcot, but life has many surprises to offer to the unsuspected, and one big surprise was to come up and help complete a perfect day.

Passing through Slough I was back in the tender with a coal pick moving out some choice lumps to help with the duff. I had cleared out behind the tool box and was scraping away under the fire iron rack when I spotted a shovel handle. It was not possible to move it as it was jammed in under two prickers, a fire bar and fire dropping shovel, so I came out from my hole, lifted out all the fire irons on to the tender then went back behind the tool box for another go.

This time I was successful and was able to remove a rusty, dirty old shovel.

Somehow I had a feeling about that shovel. I placed it behind the tool box then splashed a bit more duff round *Trematon Castle's* firebox. Even at our easy pace she had to be attended to, and the Fireman's motto is 'a little and often'.

The fire taken care of, I returned to the discovered shovel, giving it a good swill-off with the coal watering pipe, then wiping the shaft with some cotton waste, and sure enough I found burnt into the shaft the initials "L.J."

Leonard had viewed all this activity with detached interest. He was deep in his own thoughts enjoying a sentimental return of a golden age, his Mate had found a dirty old shovel and from the preparations he had made in cleaning it off he intended to use it.

With my long reach I found that I could slide that shovel with its extended shaft into the coal, lift it out and place the coal in the firebox while sitting on my seat; not that it could be carried out for long, but long enough to make a point. We were near Maidenhead and Len was on the second verse of 'Men of Harlech' when he noticed how I was firing. The singing came to an abrupt stop, he shot off his seat, grabbed that shovel, and with amazement written all over his face he kept repeating "You've found my bloody shovel, you've found my bloody shovel!".

Truth is indeed stranger than fiction.

Len was absolutely delighted. If the signalman had looked into the cab as we ran under his window he would have thought there were a couple of lunatics on the footplate; we were holding hands and dancing round and round.

With the discovery of that shovel I was informed that as I was completely familiar with the road between Reading and Swindon I would be the Driver of *Trematon Castle,* and God help me if I knocked her about.

We carried on towards Reading on the down relief line and at Reading East Main the Distant signal was at caution and remained so, the Home Starting signal dropping as we approached. Our speed had dropped to walking pace as we drifted through the station, with the 3.55pm Paddington to Fishguard roaring through on the down main, but surprise, surprise, as the express cleared Reading West Junction the points came over and our signals came off for the down main line. We were going to have a run at last.

Len came over to my side his fingers itching to get hold of his old shovel, while I crossed to the Driver's side and took over.

The cut-off was at 45% where we had drifted through the station, so I gave her a little steam and then looked back along the line of coaches to see the last one through the crossover. My moment of glory had come. I was 17 years and a few months, on the main line driving not just any old 'Castle', but the pride of the stud, 5020 *Trematon Castle.*

I opened her on to the second valve of the regulator and from the feel of her running I began to slowly wind her back a half turn at a time until she was back on 25% valve cut-off.

No ambling along now, this was the real stuff, and she began to get into her stride as only a 'Castle' can, the speedometer swinging from side to side until it settled at a steady 50mph.

Len came over and had a look; he advised a bit more on the regulator and to wind her back another couple of notches. Within a mile the speed had climbed to 60mph, we were beginning to fly. Len had removed his cloth cap and overall jacket; he was out of condition after six months as a Driver, but he was still an expert with a shovel; the steam pressure was steady at 225lbs and the exhaust injector singing away as in the old days. We swept through Pangbourne and on to the water troughs at Goring picking up 2000 gallons in one minute, then we began to draw alongside a goods train running on the down relief, the train that had held us back between Old Oak Common and Reading.

This train was rattling along at a good pace so we ran side by side for some miles, and as we drew level with the engine I could see that they were Didcot men on board. It was time to make a noise—I could see that the Fireman was Big Harold's Mate.

To meet my 'Old Chap' out on the road was always a pleasant encounter but to pass him while driving a 'Castle' was a treat not to be missed. Both whistle chains were pulled, making the most unholy row and as he looked across we held up a piece of string; the implication was plain enough—we could give him a tow!

My being his son made no difference, the reply was two fingers in the Churchillian manner! We had been rebuffed, our display of good manners rejected, but what else could you expect from a common old goods train?!

Big Harold picked up the coal watering pipe and tried to squirt water over the gap between us but the wind pressure was too great and much to our delight, he received some of it back. We gave him a final blast on the whistle, then swept majestically on.

Approaching Moreton we could see the Distant signal for Didcot East Junction at caution, and with this situation in sight I at once could feel all the frustration the main line men endure from a signal check. Here we were, running like the wind behind an express and some 'nit' of a signalman had decided to allow a movement across the junction in front of us. We pulled long and hard on the whistle chain, as if by doing so we could blow the signal off, but it remained at caution.

I closed the regulator, knocked down the clip on the reverser and wound her down to the 45 mark, then gave her a short sharp touch on the vacuum brake. The result was instantaneous, as 124 brake-blocks bit into the wheels; it was as if a giant hand had caught hold of the last coach and was holding us back. The speed dropped so quickly I had to open the large ejector and blow the brakes off again.

As they came off the inner Distant signal dropped off and we were away again, but the run had been knocked out of her. We were working hard as we passed Didcot East Junction Box. We gave them a blast on the whistle but in such circumstances signalmen remain shadowy figures behind the glaze of the windows: we were ignored. This came home to me in later years when I too was a signalman in a large box, but that is another story. *Trematon Castle* settled down again in her unflurried manner and the miles sped by until we sighted the Distant signal at caution for Highworth. It looked as if our fears were right; we ran on towards Swindon down the middle road and came to a stand at the end of the platform.

A Severn Tunnel Junction crew were waiting to relieve us and take the train on to Newport, then *Trematon Castle* would run 'light' to Cardiff Shed. Leonard decided to remain with her and spend a night at home. It was a shame Control had taken us off as we had looked forward to going through Severn Tunnel together, but there was another day. I said my farewells to Len and with reluctance climbed down from that lovely engine to catch a train back to Didcot.

The sequel came the next day when we booked on. Len told me that after I had left *Trematon Castle* he placed the shovel up in the corner so that the new Fireman had to use the original shovel. Just outside Cardiff Len's shovel 'accidentally' fell off, right opposite his allotment, and he had to get his old bike out to go and see if it had damaged any of his spring cabbages. That shovel ended up in a good home.

The rest of the week we came down to earth with a bump, covering local goods and shunting jobs, and on the Saturday we were shunting out Wantage Road Station goods yard when Big Harold came by on a brand new engine just out of Swindon Works. We were on a little 0-6-0 L.M.S. Engine; it was time to hide. The 'Old Chap' was never one to let things pass, he could remember as far back as Wednesday and he had a very long length of string ready. It was coiled round and knotted and, as cool as a cucumber, he slowed right down and tossed it right on to our footplate. The French have the right word for such a situation, "Touché!"

Number four link continued to increase in numbers of crews with the war traffic building up so that the number of men away from home was equal to the 'home grown' product. It was decided to make number four link into a weekend link to give the lads a chance to get home more frequently. We were all working long hours and to give up a few rostered free weekends was little enough to help our mates. It meant I would have to leave Leonard, but he was due to return to Cardiff soon anyway, so I moved up into number three link.

This link covered much the same as number four in the way of goods working, but it also had the Didcot, Newbury, Winchester and Southampton Branch, both passenger and goods working.

Now this Branch was either loved or loathed, and I loved it, taking to it like a duck takes to water.

I was fortunate to know it before the alterations that began in August came about, and doubly fortunate in my Driver Ralph Painton.

4

The week before I was to join Ralph I filled a sick vacancy in the passenger link. This was the 3.45pm Didcot to Paddington, returning with the 7.50pm Paddington to Didcot. It was a nice little turn stopping all stations to Slough, then fast to Paddington; the return was much the same, fast to Slough then all stations to Didcot. Booking on time was 2.30pm for off shed at 3.30pm, but I was climbing up on our engine at 2.00pm. I liked plenty of time in preparation.

The engine booked was 6923 but without name-plates — (she was named *Croxteth Hall* after the War) — due to a shortage of brass, so it was said; perhaps the brass was needed for those great injector handles on the L.M.S. Class 8F they were building at Swindon. With or without a name she was a fine engine, and just as well too; my Mate for the week was Bill Darby, and he had a reputation of being a 'hard hitter'.

With this in mind I built up a good fire so that when we backed on to our ten coaches on Number 5 Platform I had plenty of steam, fire, and water. The Guard was on Bill's side, so he would take the 'right away'. At 3.42pm the road was set "up relief" to Didcot East Junction, then "up main line". The signals dropped off, and we were ready to go.

I expected Bill to lift the regulator with his left hand when we started off, but not a bit of it; he walked over to my side, turned his back on me, caught hold of the regulator in both hands and pushed it right up into the cab roof. Only a Great Western "Hall" would stand such treatment; she took off like a scalded cat without one trace of a slip, and my carefully prepared fire had great holes torn out of it.

Passing Moreton I began to fire her as Bill wound the lever back, but he snapped down the clip at 35% cut off. It was going to be a hairy trip. My small lumps of coal never touched the fire, they went over the brick arch, through the tubes, out of the chimney and back down onto the tender again! The blast from the exhaust was something to be heard; I half expected to see the bricks fly out of Moreton Bridge as we passed underneath.

He shut off early for Cholsey, so I had a chance to regain on the boiler. There was only one way to fire for Bill and that was to keep piling it in, and if the lumps of coal were big enough to go through the fire hole so much the better, at least they stopped in long enough to burn. For all that, though, Bill was a kindly man, even if his method of driving made sure of no unemployment in the South Wales coal pits, and I was to enjoy my week with him.

I can remember with pleasure that first short, sharp, burst of fast-running between Slough and Paddington. We came up to Southall with the chimney kicking up one hell of a racket, hanging on the whistle chain as we approached the long bridge preceding the station. Passengers packed on the platform receded like waves on the sea-shore as we burst under the bridge, and we looked back along the train to see the dust and newspapers flying, with hands grasping desperately at hats of all shapes. Bill looked over at me with a grin on his face, he knew what was making me laugh, he had seen hats go flying before.

We ran into Paddington on time, where my education into the so-called 'weaker sex' was to begin. I was a well brought-up simple country boy who had been taught that ladies were ladies. I knew there were the other kind, but being a clean living lad I had no contact with that other kind. My innocence was to be shattered by an accident.

I lit the flare lamp and walked 'ound the frame to light the headlamps. This job done I blew out the flare lamp and jumped down on to the platform with one headlamp in my hand to place on the tender bracket.

I had timed it just right; the passengers we had brought with us were tearing past like they do at Paddington, always in a hurry.

One of these passengers was a young lady of ample proportions; she had a bosom that made the lads look twice, and covering this bosom was a spotless white blouse.

As I landed on the platform the dirty charred paraffin soaked stump of the flare lamp went right across that white-covered bosom leaving a long black streak. She stood quite still for a moment, looked at me, then at her blouse, then that bosom started to heave as bosoms do under stress, but the sound that issued from her mouth was nothing like a lady should use! She sounded off like a factory hooter, using words that were quite unbecoming! I got the impression that she was upset, and when she started to question the validity of my parents being married I knew she was upset. Poor Bill hung over the cab window helpless with laughter. The coaches were drawn off our engine so Bill blew off the brakes ready to follow; it was time to make a move. One more bit of indignity came my way; this distraught young lady(?)

said that she would report me to the Midland manager, and me a Great Western man! I was shattered. She swung round on her heels to leave and the string bag she had in the crook of her arm clouted the heavy headlamp I still had in my hand. There was a tinkle of glass and half a pint of gin cascaded on the dusty platform.

Bill, bless him, was quick off the mark. He had already started to move back. I flung the headlamp onto the footplate and leapt after it—this was one time to leave Paddington for Ranleigh Bridge turntable without a lamp on the tender bracket!

For the rest of the week when running into Paddington we took precautions not to be recognised, in railway language, 'From Tuesday to Saturday inclusive'. When we stopped at the buffers Bill would take off his cap, take out his teeth, and put on a pair of black horn-rimmed reading glasses. Each day that young lady would have a look up into the cab, but she would see an almost bald man with sunken cheeks wearing glasses and bent over a book. Bill, of course, picked this time to bring his train journal up to date. And Fireman? Well, he was standing on the frame with his back to the boiler on the blind side of the platform, so she never did see him again. That was the week I decided to grow the moustache I still wear, 30 years later.

It was a good week, and although Bill liked to hear the chimney bark he was a good Mate. Each day he would pass a remark about stopping on the return journey on the down relief at Maidenhead, and each day he would make the same mistake. We had a long train on the 7.50pm and to get it all on the platform we had to run to the extreme end. The A.T.C. ramp was positioned there, and as we were booked 10 minutes for Station work, to stop on the ramp would mean the A.T.C. bell ringing in the cab all that time. Bill never missed, much as he tried to! We would ram cotton waste round the rim of the bell, then go and sit on the platform bench. Bill would leave the small ejector open, then two minutes before departure we would climb back on board, but even two minutes with that bell ringing was a lifetime.

The only embarrassment was on the Friday evening when a small boy came along. All enginemen at some time or another meet these small boys. They were not only 'spotters' but they could give one information about the engine that even the designer did not know, such as how many times the wheels went round between Paddington and Plymouth, and how many times the engine exhausted in a mile, and this boy was no exception. He informed us with all seriousness that we had stopped on the

A.T.C. ramp and did we know that the bell was ringing. Bill looked very sad, then beckond the lad forward and whispered in his ear. He took off up the platform as if his tail was on fire, leaving Bill with a satisfied smirk on his face!

I never did find out what he said, but I can guess.

I recently saw a photograph in a railway book showing two enginemen sitting on a platform bench on the down relief at Maidenhead. The caption under the photograph was 'Resting'. True, very true. Perhaps the photographer was deaf.

I joined Ralph Painton as his Fireman on the Sunday night, and straight away was into another spot of fun. We booked on at 11.00pm for relief duties, on one of those nights that sometime crop up in May. It was like mid-winter, driving rain with a gale blowing. We were ordered to relieve a Swindon to Bordsley goods standing at west curve, so we walked down the centre yard between the wagons to escape the weather until we arrived by the shunters cabin, and there stood our train. One look and we almost turned back; the engine was a Westernised version R.O.D., No. 3007. She looked a stinker true to her class. To her credit she steamed, but not only in the boiler. Like her sisters she leaked steam everywhere; the cab dripped with condensation, and just to rub it in the coal was a mixture of dust and ovoids. We started off with the gait peculiar to the "Thirties". As described earlier, each revolution of the wheel produced a loud clang from the side rods and with each beat from the exhaust the engine would go forward, pause, then forward again; the result was that with the slackness between the engine and tender a perpetual backwards-forwards motion would set up. With all the time and money spent on designing self-trimming tenders the only true self-trimmer was on these monstrosities.

We clanked our way wearily towards Oxford spilling ovoids all over the track and covered in dust before we had reached Radley. No amount of water would keep it down, but at Oxford our discomfort was to be shared.

We pulled up the middle road after being checked by Distants from Hinksey, to receive a red light from Oxford Station North Box. Ralph stopped outside while I climbed down with the gauge lamp in my hand and set off to see what was wanted. As I entered the signal box the first person I saw was an R.A.F. Squadron Leader. The signalman explained that this officer had missed the last train to Heyford and asked if we would give him a lift.

Against regulations of course, but there are not many enginemen who have refused to give a serviceman a helping hand in wartime, and besides, he was such a picture in his number one uniform. I was sure he would fully appreciate our version of a Wellington bomber!

I helped him over to the engine with the feeble light from the gauge lamp, and guided his feet onto the steps and up onto the footplate. Introductions and explanations were made, then he produced an expensive cigarette case and handed it round; he was obviously a well brought up young man. We in turn showed good manners in offering him a light from our cigarette lighter, the gauge lamp. The little door was unclipped and the lamp turned towards him, and to show him that we, too, were gentlemen we advised him not to let the cigarette come in contact with the wick or it might spoil the taste of the smoke. He thanked us, accepted the light, then burnt his nose on the hot metal case of the gauge lamp! We were off to a good start.

To make him feel at home, Ralph and I went through a pre-take off check, opening and shutting the blow-through cock and generally creating an atmosphere of great things to come; then we set off. I settled him down on the seat on my side and started work, and by the time we had reached Wolvercote Junction we were beginning to pick them up a bit. We clattered over the Junction with our Squadron Leader looking a bit apprehensive. By the light of the fire I could see that the shine on his polished shoes was beginning to dim with coal dust. I gave the footplate and his toe-caps a wash down at the same time, then Ralph gave her a bit more on the regulator ready for the long pull up Tackley Bank.

The old engine began to shake and rattle as only a "Thirty" can. I opened the firebox doors, got down the long pricker and gave her a good pull through. When I withdrew the pricker it was almost white-hot from the tip to half-way up the handle. The R.A.F. trouser began to steam. She lifted her safety valve and blew off hard just as we passed under Kidlington road bridge. For one moment Ralph and I though we would lose our passenger as we roared through the station. He was on the point of bailing out, but it would have been a bit foolhardy without a parachute! As we topped the bank at Tackley the gale caught us straight into the cab, and whipped his cap off into the night! He gave a cry of despair. Conversation had not been possible because of the noise, but I gave him a Woodbine, patted him on the knee and managed to convey to him that worse things happen at sea!

Once over the top, Ralph shut off and we drifted down the

other side of the bank to come to a shuffling halt in Heyford Station.

In his eagerness to leave us our Squadron Leader put his foot under the damper handle, ripped the upper from the sole and landed face-down in the mixture of ovoids and wet dust! We picked him up and wiped him down with cotton waste, then helped him onto the platform.

He looked very forlorn standing there in the driving rain. He was covered in coal dust, he had lost his cap, somewhere he had lost one beautiful tan leather glove, he had a scorch mark on his trousers. He was no longer the immaculate officer who had joined us at Oxford, but true to tradition he was an officer and a gentleman. With a very refined public school accent he courteously thanked us for the lift back to his station, then he said he now had two ambitions in life where before he had only one. The first was to survive his flying operations and the war; the second was to get Ralph and myself into the air with him for just ten minutes! Somehow we got the impression that he had not enjoyed steam traction, and we watched him flap his way out of the station gate, with his shoe opening and closing like a crocodile's mouth. I expect he by-passed the guard room at Heyford R.A.F. Station and used the hole in the fence to get in. No self respecting guard would have believed his explanation for the state he was in.

Two weeks later Ralph and I were chugging gently along between Kingham and Charlbury on an old "Webb" 2676 towards Oxford. We had had a rough trip from Honeybourne up through the tunnel to Campden and were enjoying the Spring sunshine as we ambled along. A flight of Wellington bombers were making a long sweep round on the horizon, then lining up for the approach to Heyford in the east.

As they passed overhead one at a time we idly followed their progress. They were only about 200 feet up, so they were close enough for us to see them in detail. One by one they all disappeared behind the contour of the land on our left except one; we watched him gain height and circle away, then turn towards us, gradually dropping down to about 50 feet. He flew along level with us then pulled away to make a second run, but this time he throttled right down at about the same height as the first run but much closer. The small window in the pilot's cabin was open. We could see an arm extended and two fingers in the 'V' sign moving up and down, both front and rear gun turrets were pointing in our direction; our Squadron Leader was paying a call on us! We gave him a long blast on the whistle, knowing he could not hear it, but he would see the long column of steam.

It gave us a nice feeling to know he had not forgotten us, and we both hoped that he did survive the hard days ahead.

Most of the next few months were spent on the Didcot to Winchester Branch. It gave me an insight of single line working, but not for long between Didcot and Newbury, for the Branch was closed in August and the re-building began. When it re-opened for traffic in April 1943 it was double line as far as Woodhay.

This part of my firing days had three advantages. Ralph knew every inch of the Branch and as I was an apt pupil he soon had me loving it too. I found I could change a train staff at 45 to 50 mph with complete confidence, even on the darkest night. Regulation 23 states "10mph" but you can't mess about on a bank at that speed!

I was introduced to the modern version of the Dean Goods Engine, Mr. Collett's 22XX Class, and with the re-building I literally walked every inch of the Branch between Didcot and Winchester.

The "Twenty Two's" were, I think, the best engine we had for local Branch work. We had a large stud of them at Didcot loco shed, and each one of them was a good engine. There was one only that was disliked, but not because of the engine alone—that part of her was alright. This was 2252, and she was mated up with an old R.O.D. tender. The result was ridiculous, the overall picture was completely out of proportion and spoilt a fine engine.

The first trip I had with Ralph over the 'lingering die', as the Branch was known to the Didcot men, was on a Sunday morning with a special goods for Winchester.

Our engine was the old *Comet,* Number 3283, one of the "Duke of Cornwall" Class, she still retained the outside frames, a very narrow cab with a great screw reverser taking up most of the Driver's space, but for an old engine, like her sister 3254 *Cornubia* she was a good one.

Boiler pressure was only 180lbs but she would steam like the proverbial kettle, pull like a cart horse, and run like a deer. The firebox was low down on the footplate, so firing her was a bit awkward. It was almost as if one threw the coal in a hole in the floor; you had to miss the damper handles with the left hand when swinging round with the shovel, and miss the Driver's ankles with the blade.

Ralph now and again would try an old trick Drivers liked to play. Just as the shovel swung round for a planned shot to the front corner of the firebox he would stick out his foot. The result would be coal scattered all over the floorboards. Retribution would come when next the floorboards were washed down—the coal watering pipe would stray—so as soon as Ralph saw me pick up the pipe he would sit up on the reverser with his feet on the tip-up seat. Who would have thought that 20 years later Ralph would be the Driver of the last passenger train over the branch? They were happy days, but with the amount of engineering material we began to transport it was obvious that the alterations about to begin were to be major ones. The Branch was to become part of a planned strategy for the invasion of Europe.

In August 1942 we began working engineering trains until we were sick of the sight of them. Our old Branch was being ripped apart, and it was a pleasure to have a week away on the main line, although even that could be spoilt as a result of the 'block'.

With air raids going on it was a common occurrence to be blocked back by Control, so that it sometimes took as much as 10 to 12 hours to work a train from Didcot to Reading. Engines were on the road weeks overdue for boiler washout, superheaters and tubes leaked, the coal was bad, and duties of sixteen, eighteen and twenty hours were worked frequently; but enough has been written about the bad days, this is a book written about the good days, and human nature being what it is it is better to recall days that gave pleasure. The year 1942 gave us a new and exciting engine to work, with the introduction of the 2–8–0 Freight on loan from the U.S.A. Transportation Corps. The Great Western loco-men took them straight to their hearts; they were great ugly locomotives, sporting a maze of plumbing all over the boiler and with every bit of motion exposed, and were the direct opposite to the clean lines of a Western engine. Perhaps it was the fact that they were so opposite that gave them their charm, and perhaps, too, it was the comfort.

I can still remember the wonderment on climbing aboard one for the first time. The first impression was one of greatness, everything looked twice as large; it seemed a massive boiler front which extended back into a large cab, but each side of that boiler was an armchair upholstered to such a degree that it was obvious they were meant to be sat in.

This was something new indeed after the tip-up wooden seat we were used to. We tried them for size and found them very comfortable, but the proof would be in the eating. The crew we relieved explained the controls to us, but with the adaptability of all enginemen we could see that we would have no trouble in handling this monster.

We stood on the up middle road at Swindon Station. A large crowd of passengers had gathered on the platform to examine this strange new engine while we waited for signals, and they were in for a surprise! I opened the firebox doors and splashed half a dozen shovelfulls of coal round that great square box, and as the needle climbed up to blowing off the end of the world came! Instead of a gentle whisper at the safety valve to warn one of pressure about to escape, those valves lifted with such a roar that we both though for one moment that the boiler had exploded. I had never heard such a roar of escaping steam before, and then as suddenly as they had gone off the valves closed with a 'pop'.

I looked over to Ralph to see the colour come back into his face. He looked as shaken as I did, I could hear my heart thudding. We had been taken for a ride! I thought that the draught was a bit fierce in the firebox, an I could now see why—the Swindon Fireman had given the blower half a turn! Ralph and I looked over the side; there was not a passenger left on the platform near us, the last one was still running towards the far end! And the Swindon crew? They were about four wagons back, the Driver with a grin on his face, but the Fireman was sitting on the ground absolutely helpless with laughter!

Well, two can play at that game. We would try it on the next crew, and so it would go on until everyone was initiated to the peculiarities of the Yank engines.

The gauge glass was a flat Pyrex effort set in a frame showing the water black. She was three quarters full, so after one experiment with the injector we were ready to 'blow up' for the signal.

Ralph gave a pull on the whistle and we had our second surprise. It was a full-blooded, honest-to-goodness American railroad bellow. In that one moment we were transported away from the flat plains of green England to the vast expanse of the great American West. We were the Baltimore and Ohio, the Union Pacific all rolled into one. On shutting one's eyes one could almost see the arrows flying and hear the whoops of the Indians.

We pulled gently away to get the feel of her, Ralph set the regulator on the ratchet and let her take her time as he linked her up, and passing Highworth Box I placed a dozen shovelfulls round her firebox.

It was then that I found that the arm-chair on the Fireman's side was to be used after all. I sat down all the way to Challow, where I put a bit more round her again and put the injector on for a bit, then sat down again to Didcot. We had never seen anything like it; there seemed no end of power in that boiler, and at such little effort.

With a light load and with the up road from Swindon in our favour it did make for an easy trip, but later as we had more and more Yanks allocated to the Great Western we found them to be capable of any task set for them. There was the unfortunate accident at Honeybourne, where one of them blew a main steam pipe, killing the enginemen, that gave us all a few moments of concern, and as they aged they got a bit rough on the motion, but for all that we were well satisfied with them. The one part of them I did dislike was the sand box. This was situated on the top of the boiler between the whistle and chimney, and I can well remember topping one up with sixteen buckets of sand. How many buckets they took when empty was an experience I was happy to forego.

However, this first trip was a very pleasant one. I ran the boiler down a bit as we passed between Wantage Road and Steventon so that I could put the injector on and keep her from blowing off as we waited for relief. It was now our turn to scare the pants off the unsuspecting enginemen!

Our relief came almost at once, and we climbed down leaving the engine in the up loop at Foxhall Junction. Needless to say, the blower was left on half a turn!

We had just crossed over the Junction when we heard the bellow of her whistle, and were walking up the foot-path between the up relief and the provender stores sidings towards Didcot West Box when she came creeping by. Like Ralph at Swindon, this Driver was taking her away gently to get the feel of her. Her Fireman was standing on the running plate between the engine and tender with a cup of tea in his hand when she blew off; he dropped the cup as if was red hot, and the Driver jerked back his head and thumped it against the back support of the cab! Like the crew we had relieved at Swindon, Ralph and I hung on to each other, helpless with laughter. Vengeance is sweet.

These safety valves proved somewhat of a problem during the next few months, causing damage to the elaborate overhang of some stations, and blowing out signal lamps all over the system. I had one blow off on the up main line coming through Banbury Station, which took half of the footbridge with it. (Banbury needed a new station, so part of the demolition took place a little early). Orders were soon distributed to all locomotive sheds, drawing attention to the rule book whereby the emission of smoke or steam is prohibited. The message from Management was plain enough—knock it off boys, you've had your fun.

The winter of 1942 saw us hard at work on the Winchester Branch with the engineering trains. I say hard at work with tongue in cheek to some extent; there were of course some hard duties but the majority of the work was very undemanding.

There were up to eight ballast trains working between Didcot and Winchester taking three crews to each train. The early shift would prepare the engine and leave with a ballast train for the site, or go light engine; the middle shift would go by bus to the site, and relieve the early shift who would return by bus; the late shift would relieve the middle shift, then take the engine back to shed.

All shifts had a bus ride either coming or going, but the 'plum' job was the middle shift, particularly if the work was south of Whitchurch, as this meant a three hour ride over the Berkshire Downs and into the Hampshire countryside, five hours on the engine, then a nice ride home on the bus again.

As all the train services in this area were suspended, the travelling public used the buses, but there was one unpublished goods train in each direction early morning and late at night. Working this train had its moments, as at some places the single line token was suspended as total occupation was in force, at others the points were clipped and we shuttled over from up to down, or crossed over where none existed a few hours before. However, in spite of all the difficulties throughout a long winter the re-building was completed without any accidents—well, almost.

At Highclere, before the alterations, the signal box was on the Down side, and the single line instruments in the booking office on the Up Side. The Signalman would place the token in the post for the next section then retire to the office. It was then the practice of Firemen to pick up the new token and by skillful aim throw the old token through the doorway of the booking office, where the Signalman would place it in the instrument without getting up from his chair. Ralph had taught me how to throw this token, and being a darts player I soon found I could throw this heavy piece of metal through the door each time without adding any more marks to the scarred door post.

On the very last day of the old working before the new signal box was brought into use, the inevitable happened. I threw the token as the Signalman walked out of the door!

For a man in his sixties he moved quicker then he had moved for years—he would have done credit to that most eminent of dancers, Fred Astaire. His footwork was a work of art, but his language was not, it was most unbecoming for a man who I knew was a sidesman in the local church!

My diary shows that from Monday October 5th to Saturday October 10th I was with Ralph on the Winchester ballast. "Booked on at 7.15 am, bused to Winchester; worked with 'Bulldog' 3448 *Kingfisher,* then bused home, booked off at 6.15 pm." So it was an 11 hour day and a 66 hour week. My pay was £3.19.3d. On this middle shift that week we had one driver who was working the Whitchurch section. He was an expert in catching rabbits, and with the meat ration on the short side he was in demand. To meet this demand he would bring to work with him a couple of nets and a ferret, and set to work on the banks of Larks Barrow Hill Cutting.

He was a fat man, so with the assumption that a couple of pounds extra to his figure would not be noticed, he would undo a button on his shirt, pop the ferret in, tighten up his belt and sit down.

He always chose the back seat of the bus, so the little ferret would lie along his stomach, warm and comfortable, and go to sleep. At Newbury we were joined by a large overbearing lady passenger who made it quite clear that the railway was going to the dogs when passengers had to share a public vehicle with dirty old engine drivers. She sat opposite our mate, viewing him with distaste all the way to Litchfield, until the back wheel of the bus dropped into a hole in the road and woke up little Fred. He stuck his sharp little nose out the shirt front, his whiskers on each side of his dear little face twitching with anticipation. The large lady and ferret looked into each other's eyes for some seconds, then she let out a screech that sounded just like a hot axle box! Fred disappeared back into the warm like quicksilver.

From her description of the animal she had seen it could have been a kangaroo. It took us all the way to Whitchurch to convince her that she had suffered an illusion, probably due to something she ate, and the jerking of the bus had brought it on! We advised her to see her doctor.

As the work progressed we could see that the freight trains we would be handling in the next few years would be of main line proportions, for we noticed the length of the passing loops, and this would mean big engines on the Branch. At times, the engineering work would allow us to be stationary for lengthy periods, so we would take it in turns to leave the engine and go and examine our new Branch. In this way, little by little, we walked the whole distance between sections.

We both looked at the drop down from Litchfield to Whitchurch with some misgiving. The ruling gradient was 1 in 106 falling, to end up with some throw off points just to the south of Whitchurch Station. It did not take long to work out that a Twenty Eight, L.M.S. 8F, and the big Yank engines would be loaded with up to 46 Number Ones, and with a 20 ton brake van at the back we should be running down that bank with best part of a thousand tons on the move, with every chance of landing up in the road leading to Whitchurch Town.

A mental note was made to make sure we had full sand boxes when the crunch came.

By the middle of April 1943 it had all been completed, we were ready for anything, and it was not long in coming.

The American Army and Air Force arrived at Newbury and Sutton Scotney via courtesy of the Great Western Railway and the Didcot – Winchester Branch. We ran troop trains for weeks, filling up the South of England with Yanks, and with them came a new invention—instant coffee. Whenever we arrived at the discharging station, we would be loaded up with 'K' rations, long waxed cardboard boxes stamped 'Breakfast' or 'Dinner'. Inside these was a wealth of food, cheese, biscuits, tinned meat, four Chesterfield or Camel cigarettes; and half a dozen little packets of brown powder, with instructions to empty one packet into a cup, add boiling water and stir; the result was coffee such as we had never tasted before. In these 'K' rations were also a dozen soft toilet tissues, to be used for obvious reasons. They made a pleasant change from an old service book cut in half, drilled in one corner for the string, and hung in a corner. It was said that the Yanks had ice cream too, but we did not see any; we were very satisfied with powdered coffee and nice soft toilet paper.

We ran one American troop train that summer with our old *Comet*. The train of eight coaches arrived in the up gully at Didcot East Junction from Birkenhead Docks, the engine came off and *we* backed on, to ribald comments from the troops watching the operation.

From their point of view I suppose we did look a bit comic backing on to couple up, with our tall chimney, steam dome, and curved splashers joining the small open cab. There were many comparisons made between *Comet* and the *General Grant*, so Ralph and I set out to show these Yanks a thing or two. All troop trains were allowed plenty of time in running, (in fact main line running was restricted to a shadow of pre-war years), and we might be called "That little old locomotive" in a deep Southern-state American accent, but they would change their minds by the time we arrived at Sutton Scotney.

We pulled away and clattered over the junction towards the Branch, letting her take her time until we were under the Hagbourne road bridge and into the bank heading for Upton. I had a deep solid bed of fire, so she had plenty to bite on.

Normally Ralph would have started to link her up, he was the most gentle of Drivers, but we were both a bit upset, and if Ralph wanted to work her hard that was all right by me. We stormed up that bank so fast that the Upton signalman was standing on the steps of the box to watch us. Through the station we roared and pounded on up the bank. By the time we had reached the three-arch bridge and three-quarters of the way to the top, we had made the fastest time ever. I had had the exhaust injector on all the way from Didcot, and had not once stopped firing. Then we were over the top and on the way down the drop as far as Hampstead Norris. We rocketed through Compton, and bucked and swayed through Hamstead Norris at such a speed that the 1 in 106 climb to Hermitage was a mear pimple, but we had to ease down a bit for the drop down the bank into Newbury—we had made such fast time there might be some questions asked if we arrived there too early.

We were booked for water at Newbury, so after we had stopped on the middle road I put the bag in the tank, then nipped into the signal box for a quiet word with the signalman.

We arranged for him to telephone ahead to all boxes as far as Sutton Scotney to have the single line tokens placed in the racks, and not for the signalmen to stand on the end of the platforms with them as they normally would do. Hand-exchange of tokens had become custom and practice with the leisurely life of the Branch, but the staff were in for an example of main line running to brighten up the quiet stations. Ralph's instruction during the past months were soon to bear fruit; I had a heavy leather glove all ready to place on my left hand, for there would be no 10mph on these token exchanges.

We 'blew up' for the road, the home and starter dropped and we were away, building up speed towards Enbourne Junction. Ralph eased down a bit as we turned left off the main line, but as soon as we had passed Enbourne Box he opened her up again for the 1 in 106 climb to Woodhay.

We were now on the last bit of double line. I collected the token as we climbed at 30mph towards Highclere. The exchange was made there for Burghclere, and even at 30mph the heavy hoop stung through the leather glove. Then came that little bit of road described in my first firing trip over the branch; we swooped down the bank, shot through the bridge at the bottom and were away up the other side.

News of our record run had brought half the population out to see us through Burchclere but speed was not so high, for we still had a short bit of bank to climb. It was about a mile south of Burghclere that the real run of speed would begin, right down to Sutton Scotney ten miles further on. Through Litchfield we were on a falling gradient of 1 in 106, and we went through like the "Bristolian". The token which I threw onto the post went round and round like a spinning top, and when I picked up the token for the Whitchurch Section the speed was such that it flew back, hitting the tender with such a thump that it knocked out a great lump of paint, but I hung on to it much to Ralph's relief; he told me later he though he had overdone it a bit through Litchfield.

Down into Whitchurch we flew, but Ralph gave her a touch on the brake, the exchange was made, and we tore on towards the next station, Sutton Scotney. The old *Comet* stood there sizzling, while the American troops piled out. Ralph was going round placing his hand on the axle boxes; the *Comet* had been run faster than she had ever run before, but all was well. She started to blow off as if to tell us she could do it all over again.

One of the American sergeants came along to us and said he would never have believed it possible for an engine such as ours to run like that unless he had been on board. He told us that we had achieved something that would go down in the Regimental History Book; we had stopped the game of 'craps' in his platoon, and instead they were laying bets on me missing the next token, and whether or not the side rods would fly off.

He himself was an ex New York Central man, so he had some previous knowledge of locomotive running. He patted his tunic pocket with appreciation, for he had backed me catching all the tokens, then he handed over a carton as a gesture of thanks—a few cigarettes, as he termed 500 Chesterfields.

An officer came up and told him to get a move on. The reply was to shock us; the 'Lootenant was to stop beating his gums'. No salutes, no recriminations, in fact the 'Lootenant' looked chastened for disturbing us. Our Sergeant did eventually get a move on as requested, but only just in time to scramble up on the tailboard of the last lorry pulling out of the station yard.

No Goddammed Officer was telling him what to do!

We were booked to run to Winchester with the empty coaches, and then turn the engine back to Didcot, but as it was a nice day we decided to run round the train and go back tender-first. We were in no hurry, in fact we were very pleased with ourselves, and anyway, Winchester turntable was no picnic. It was fitted in the days of small engines, so the only way to turn was to run the engine over the table, lift up some heavy ramps with a crowbar, and then back the tender up these ramps. It was impossible to balance an engine perfectly, but once she was on, the table was moved by turning two great mangle-wheels round and round. It was the most efficient method of stripping off waistcoat buttons I have ever seen; sooner or later everyone was caught by those handles. They would come round and under, then up inside the garment, and then it was either over the top with you, or lose the buttons! Thank goodness for weak cotton!

We ambled back, smoking our Chesterfields and discussing the run. The Yanks now had a different outlook on Limey enginemen, but they were a good lot of lads, and generous to a fault.

South of Newbury was a restricted area right across the south coast, and security was tight. All troop movements were top secret, and even we did not know until booking on where we would be sent when handling these trains. But in spite of all the precautions taken to ensure secrecy there was a leak in the system. The local children knew all. Their intelligence service must have been the envy of every army commander; they would line the fields each side of the station, and as soon as they were spotted by the Yank lads the windows would come down and a shower of sweets, chocolate, chewing gum and tins of Spam for Mum would come flying out, to the delighted shrieks of the children.

I can't ever remember an American troop train leaving without the children being there. How those Yanks loved our kids.

Ralph and I saw the start of the heavy freight traffic to Southampton on the Branch, then the Management formed a special link of twenty Drivers and Firemen to work these supply trains. I was one of the Firemen who applied to be in this link, while Ralph took on a job he richly deserved—he was appointed to Shift Foreman on the Shed.

I kicked about for several weeks waiting to be mated up with another Driver, and spent that time on loan to Newbury.

There was no shed there; instead half a dozen sets of men worked Engines supplied by Didcot. It was my good fortune to spend the first week on night duty on the Newbury Town pilot engine with a real gentleman for a Mate, Charlie Darrle-Smith who in later years became a Locomotive Inspector. I keep coming across his name in railway literature, and read of his exploits with interest, although I expect he is now retired and I hope in good health.

The second week was spent as a member of the American Army, firing a diminutive little tank engine on Newbury race course for a very large Driver. The Americans had turned the race course into a vast supply depot, with miles of railway lines laid down. They were short of Firemen, so I had a wonderful week with them. I have the very cherished memory of passing the winning post up the straight opposite the grandstand on Newbury race course on a steam locomotive!

That week I used to go home loaded with all the food I could carry. My American Driver had taken one look at my brown wartime bread with its thin sliver of cheese and had thrown it in the firebox. Then he had taken me off to the canteen for 'chow'. The first meal was an eyeopener; the ham on the plate was a quarter of an inch thick, covered with two eggs 'sunnyside up'. To go with it were waffles, or as we would call them pancakes, topped with a thick brown syrup, and then to wash it all down was a pint of American coffee. Each evening he would load me up with tins of Spam, sausage-meat, butter, and cheese, and at the end of the week my underclothes, shirts, and boots ended up in the firebox and I was kitted out with my American Army clothes. I had two pairs of boots which lasted for years. They were made of soft leather, uncoloured and in their natural state, so they could be dyed black or brown. As for cigarettes, I had enough to last me for months.

I can't remember that Driver's name now except that his first name was Charlie, and that he was a locomotive man from Milwaukee, but I can remember he couldn't bring himself to call me "Harold" or "Mate"; I was 'Al'.

At the end of that fortnight I was back at Didcot and all ready to start on the Southampton run, but it was a gradual build up for there was still plenty to do on the Main Line.

I had another week spare and spent it in Foxhall up loop in charge of trains blocked back. There would be as many as four or five trains in the loop, all with engines in steam at the head of each one, and by the time I had worked my way back to the last one, topping up the boiler and firebox, it was time to walk back to the first one and start all over again.

I had on one of the trains an old friend, 2330 *Cudworth*, one of the "Remembrance" Class from the old London, Brighton, and South Coast Railway. As she was so low on coal and water I threw out her fire; she was so full up with muck from being on the road for so long that it took me all night to complete the job in between looking after the other engines, but it was nice to be able to take care of an old friend.

The next week I had a Mate again, Jack Thomas, one of the Welsh Drivers. No more messing about spare, now we could get on with the job of running trains again.

5

Jack had been at Didcot for some time, so he was no stranger to the area covered by Didcot Shed. He was proud of the fact that he had started his career in railway work with the old Taff Vale Railway, and although now a Great Western man the Taff held pride of place. Thus the Winchester Branch held no problems, for Jack had been weaned on banks and heavy coal trains up and down the Welsh Valleys.

I worked with him from May 1943 until February 1944 and found, like all the Welsh lads, he was a grand person to know.

With Jack I never used the tender hand-brake, as he was a master with the vacuum brake and on our first trip together he asked me to leave all the braking to him. The normal practice was for the fireman to wind on the hand-brake when the Driver shut off and bring the buffers of the wagons up together, and then, as the speed began to fall off, to gently unwind again; on bank working, however, the hand-brake went on hard as soon as the engine stuck her head downhill. But Jack would give the engine five inches of vacuum and take the train down the steepest bank with a nonchalance that had to be seen.

He never worried about anything. We had our rough trips like other men, with poor coal, dirty fires, and leaking tubes, the steam pressure could be down so low we would just be able to keep going, and the water level in the boiler bobbing in the bottom nut, but Jack would give a grin, hand me a cigarette, and somehow we would get over the situation. If it did get too bad, then we would do the same as all the others — stop for a brew up. Then, as soon as we had recovered steam pressure and water level, we would be off again. We always reckoned that if the engine needed a rest then so did we, so the tea can went in the firebox as soon as we had stopped.

Our first week on the Branch went off with a bang — literally! We were booked on the 4.30 am. Didcot to Winchester Goods. This duty was a double-headed job. Two of Collett's "Twenty Two's" were coupled with a full load for Newbury where the front engine would come off and work at Newbury as the pilot engine, while the second, or train engine, would carry on with a reduced load as far as Burghclere or Litchfield, and change over with the Winchester stopping passenger and work back to Didcot, the Winchester men going forward with the Goods. It was a pleasure to have this duty, as we had regular engines and we could be sure of an early finish, which made a change from some of the twelve and fourteen hour duties of the previous weeks.

That 4.30am start out of Didcot up yard was a sight to see. We would pull gently away until we were clear of Didcot east junction points, then both engines would be opened up.

A Twenty Two worked with a small regulator opening and short valve cut off could make quite a racket from the chimney, but two working together was enough to wake up the whole town!

On a clear summer morning as we passed through Upton station we could look back down towards Didcot and see where we had left the Yard for there would be a smoke trail for about four miles, then we would be into the cutting and going hammer and tongs towards Churn, showering sparks and cinders high into the air.

Hampstead Norris was the worst place, as if the train was a long one it would be on four levels between the north of the station and the start of the bank, so we would both ease down until we felt the slight tug as the guard wound his brake on, (this would indicate that all the couplings were tightly stretched out and there was no fear of a division in the train), then we could open up again and blast our way up to Hermitage.

On the Tuesday we had the aforementioned Bang. Our train engine was 2222, and the front one a Didcot "Dukedog", 3208. We coupled up at the Shed signal on a wet morning, and as the signal came off made our way up towards the stop blocks to clear the points into the yard. Speed was only walking pace, but when our mate on the front engine applied the brakes that old "Dukedog" picked up her feet on the wet rails and we slammed into the blocks. With a combined weight of around 180 tons it was a hell of a wallop; it brought the coal tumbling down all over the floor boards. My first thought was for the brick arch, but that was all right. Jack was swearing because our can of tea had gone flying.

We climbed down and went forward to see what damage was caused. The chaps on the front engine were all right, and a look round both engines showed that they, too, were undamaged; but the stop blocks were a sorry sight, as both fishplates were broken, the wooden beam of the block was a mass of firewood, and we had shifted the whole lot forward about three feet.

We backed down the yard on to our train, leaving the mess for the platelayers to clear up, then carried on with the business of belting away up towards Upton.

Although late away by about half an hour over the stop block incident, we made good time, and with only a little station work at Newbury we left early and got as far as Whitchurch before meeting the stopper and changing over.

We had a normal run back, arriving in the No. 1 bay platform on time. Looking over to our right we could see that while we had been away the platelayers had been busy; they had rebuilt the shattered stop block, and were putting the final coat of red paint on to the block. Our station work completed we backed right over to the Newbury bridge on the branch and waited for the road to be set for the carriage sidings. Then, after a down main fast had gone through, we made our way over the junction. Once in the sidings the station pilot came on the back and pulled our coaches off, and we were ready for Shed.

Back up the sidings we crept, towards the stop blocks where the platelayers were packing up their tools and wiping the paint brushes. We had no vacuum, as the pipe had not been placed back on the plug when the coaches were drawn off, so Jack operated the steam brake as we drew near to the blocks. There was a loud bang from underneath the engine, and at once we both knew what had happened—the steam pipe had broken. There was no time to wind on the tender hand brake: we slammed into those stop blocks, and all the hard work of the last few hours by those platelayers was undone!

The ganger in charge was a churchman like the signalman at Litchfield who had jumped about so smartly when I had thrown that token, but *he* did not swear until Jack made an undiplomatic remark when we were examining the damage we had caused. All that Jack had said was that we were the only engine at Didcot that had two nice red buffers! The paint was still wet, and the buffers did look smart with a shiny coat of paint on them, but that statement was the straw that broke the camel's back. The Ganger used words that he thought he had forgotten: Jack and I agreed afterwards that he must have spent his youth in the Navy, and in foreign ports!

Looking back on it now, I can see he had good reason to swear. It had been a dirty wet morning, and we hadn't helped matters by knocking down his stop blocks. It should have been done in the afternoon for then he would have been paid overtime for the repair, which would have made the job sweeter!

The rest of the week went off as it should with no incidents.

Then we found that we would be back on the Branch the next week, as we were booked relief for the Southampton supply trains.

At 11.00am on the Monday morning we relieved a Long Marsdon to Eastleigh in the up gully. The engine was 2818, now preserved in the Bristol City Museum. She was one of the originals without the outside steam pipes, having been built in 1905 and somehow escaped some of the modifications that had been applied to a lot of the "Twenty Eights". She was in fine fettle, just out of Swindon Shops after a heavy overhaul. We used to refer to the type of repair she had undergone as 'soled and heeled'. The repairs carried out at Swindon were major, so the engine was as good as new, except that no paint-work was re-newed, the smokebox and chimney only receiving a coat of black paint.

We pulled out of the gully and across the junction without any trouble with a full load of 46 number ones, all open coal wagons full of jerry cans filled with petrol.

Jack put his left foot on the large bolt that comes right through the reverser quadrant and pulled back on the great reversing lever to notch her up, but she was so tight on the valves that he had to shut off before he could move the lever. It was a good sign, she was steam tight everywhere. The exhaust injector began to sing with a sweetness that was a joy to listen to as I put it on to maintain the boiler. I fired her for about a mile, then sat down on the seat to enjoy the view.

We went spanking up the bank towards Upton. It was going to be one of those perfect days. Little did we know what was in store for us before we reached Compton.

We were halfway up the bank when we ran into a sudden rain shower. Our "Twenty Eight" picked up her heels and slipped; Jack shut off at once, then opened her up again. She slipped, again Jack shut off, then opened her up, and again she slipped. The regulator was tight so Jack had to use both hands, but try as he could he found it impossible to get her to hold the road. The exhaust injector blew out with the regulator being opened and shut, so I closed it and gave Jack a hand. As he opened her up, I worked the sand levers, but nothing would stop her slipping. It looked as if we would have to stop and part the train, and go to Compton with the front portion, then return for the rear on a Guard's wrong line order form, but there must be an answer to this persistent slipping, so I climbed down the foot-steps and had a look as Jack worked the sand levers. There was no sand on the rails.

I climbed back onto the running plate, then worked my way along the frame to the sand boxes, lifted the lid of the left-hand side box and found it full of wet sand. The right hand side was in the same condition; no wonder we couldn't stop slipping.

Our speed had now dropped to walking pace. It was touch and go. With only half a mile to the top of the bank, Jack had closed right down; we had stopped slipping, but as soon as he tried to give her a bit more steam she would pick up her heels again.

I gave her a good dozen shovel-fulls of coal to keep her firebox up. Then we thought we would try just one more thing to help her to the top. I climbed down with the shovel in my hand, ran ahead of her and started to shovel earth, ballast, chippings, and anything else that was handy, scattering it all over the rails in front of her. She followed me along, scrunching the rubbish under her wheels, but she kept going. That half a mile seemed like two, but we made it. I climbed back aboard just before we reached the top; it had been a near thing. If she had been a worn out old engine I don't think we would have made it, as the boiler and fire would have needed too much attention. We had been lucky.

Jack shut off as we passed through Churn. It was a gentle drop down now to Hampstead Norris, and we had time to take a breather; the tea can went in the firebox in double quick time. That was one of the best cups of tea we had enjoyed for a long time, and a cigarette to go with it which we both felt was well-earned.

We had no more trouble with slipping. Hampstead Norris bank was dry and she sailed up, but we were very careful descending a wet rail into Whitchurch later on. It started to rain as we ran through Litchfield, so as soon as we started the drop towards Whitchurch I wound on the tender hand-brake and when I felt her start to bite I screwed it down as far as I could. Even then we began to increase speed, so Jack had to give her a whiff of vacuum to hold her back, but we made it without ending up in the road at the bottom of the bank.

We ran without any further incident to Eastleigh goods yard, then to Shed to turn; for once the Southern Control had no back-working for us and we could go home light engine.

It was the first time we had been on Eastleigh Shed with an engine, although Jack had had a look round when he was learning the road. The planning of the Shed was first class. There was no need to go on the table as a triangle had been provided, so we used it, pulling up behind three Southern engines at the Shed signal.

I say signal, but in fact it was a ground dummy. There was no telephone to the signal box but instead a route indicator let the signalman know where the departing engine was to go.

This was a new procedure to me, so I went forward to see the Southern Fireman operate it and explain it to me. I found it a simple and straight-forward piece of equipment to use and thought that it could be of some advantage on our Sheds: in fact, it was a bit of a shock to find another railway with something better than the Great Western! I knew we had the best locomotives, but this really was something.

The indicator was in a large box. When the door was opened you were confronted by a clock with one hand. Instead of numbers the positions on the clock face showed the lines on which you could go, such as "up main", "up platform", and so on, all round the clock face. On the outside of the clock all round the rim and opposite the names on the face were small levers, all in the locked position except one, and that would be where the preceding engine had gone.

The drill now was to pull back the lever that was out, watch the hand go round the clock face, then push the lever opposite the line indicated where one wanted to go. This would be repeated on a duplicate clock in the signal box, so the signalman would know exactly where one engine at the Shed was bound for without calling him to a telephone.

The only snag I could see was that although both signalman and enginemen knew where they were heading, one dummy coming off took one to any of a dozen roads; you could come off Shed right into the path of a down express tearing through Eastleigh Station, or so it seemed, then at the last minute turn away on another line, but there was a moment of doubt when one wondered if a slip-up had been made.

Who would have thought when we left Eastleigh Shed that day on 2818 that nearly thirty years later she would be the one "Twenty Eight" chosen for preservation, and that she would return to Eastleigh for overhaul! From photographs I have seen of her since preservation they made a good job of her at Eastleigh. I am not surprised, for they are a grand lot of lads on the Southern, and on the next trip down I found that to be true.

Jack was off sick, and I had an Eastleigh trip with another Driver. This time we had one of the big American engines, Number 2573, the same number as a Dean goods engine we had at Didcot, but what a difference in engines! We had a good run down to

Robinson's R.O.D. 30xx Class. There were a 100 bought from the War Department by the Great Western after the 1914-18 War. No. 3031 as illustrated was similar to 3007 described in Chapter 4. Note the top feed and Swindon boiler, and absence of vacuum pipe. There were three ways of stopping these locomotives. a) Steam brake. b) Reverse and open regulator. c) Wind on tender handbrake and pray. They were great brutes of locomotives, with the lumbering gait of an ox. Half the coal shown on the tender of this one will end up on the ballast, caused by the slackness between engine and tender. As described in the chapter, they were the only self trimming tenders I knew as a fireman.

No. 5020 *Trematon Castle.* The beloved engine of Chapter 3. She was a credit to Canton Shed, Cardiff. Even in the dark war days with acute shortage of staff, this engine was kept in immaculate condition

No. 111 *Viscount Churchill.* The locomotive that started out as *The Great Bear* and was later re-built as a 'Castle'. I once fired this engine three days running on three different trains, a coal empty, a stopping passenger, and fast vacuum fitted freight. To me, and to other enginemen I spoke to, she never had the 'feel' of a 'Castle' about her, it might have been imagination, but something about her was alien, she steamed and pulled well enough, but she did not seem to run like a 'Castle'.

No. 2347. Standard Goods Engine, built by William Dean. These engines were known as Dean or Standard Goods engines. Some of them survived for 75 years but were replaced by the Collett 22xx class. They were wonderful little engines. No. 2573 took part in the inter-region trials in 1947. Her performance was superior to Mr. Ivatt's then new design 2-6-0, entered by the Midland. Many ended as stationary boilers at Locomotive sheds, they were simply lifted off the wheels and frames, then set down on a brick cradle. Didcot shed still has one in this condition. Note the spindle flap up for oiling spindle cups, whistles protruding from cab roof, and absence of top feed, clack boxes were mounted on the boiler inside the cab.

Note the A.T.C. camp on No. 5697, prominent in the absence of pony wheels on this class. From the amount of coal on the cab, in small lumps, it would seem that the fireman of this engine is lucky; it was usually very large lumps to go through the very small hole inside the cab.

No. 5083 *Reading Abbey*. She was a coal burner when I knew her, and like No. 4089 *Donnington Castle* and the other Castles I fired, there was no other locomotive to compare with them. The 'Castle' was I think the supreme passenger engine.

No. 4089 *Donnington Castle* at speed.

No. 3454 *Skylark*. The dear old *Skylark* of chapter 1 and 6. The old lady looks worn out, and nearing the end of her days. When I first knew her she was immaculate, her safety valve cover sparkled, her copper chimney band was burnished, and her paintwork gleamed. Of the same class as No. 3376 *River Plym* No. 3408 *Bombay* and No. 3448 *Kingfisher* she was one of the survivors of a class of 126 engines built.

No. 6162 illustrated was a passenger class loco, used for fast services on stopping passenger trains, the acceleration from the stops was very rapid indeed. Note steam heating pipe on front butter beam, used when running bunker first. One of this class 6106 is preserved at Didcot in full working order. A run on this engine is described in Chapter 5 but, as with all main line tank engines, she too, like the others, would remove skin and body moisture.

Nos. 5763 and 7777. Two examples of the pannier tank. The Great Western had over 700 of this type of engine, they were to be found all over the system. They were powerful little engines, if ever there was an example of a standard then this must be it. Both engines illustrated are fitted with steam heating pipes for passenger working. Later versions were fitted with a rounded cab and larger windows. No. 5763 has the rear door open on the bunker to catch the cool air on an abviously hot day. The bulge to the left of the bunker door is to accommodate enough clearance for the hand brake.

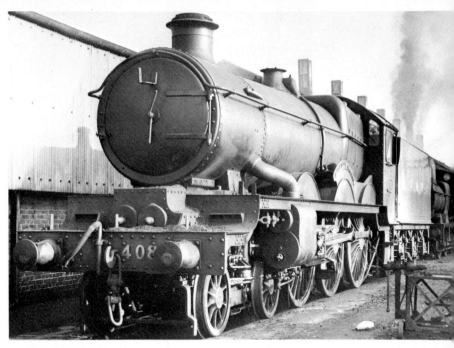

No. 4085 *Berkeley Castle*. This engine was a beauty, on the many occasions I fired her I never had one rough trip, like *Trematon Castle* she was perfection. In this illustration she is shown with the new Western tender. Note the amount of smoke box ashes on her front buffer beam. In preparation for her next run the fireman will open the smokebox, brush off the inside, then close the smokebox door up tight. It was always advisable to check where one's driver was when brushing off the ash as on a windy day those ashes would fly everywhere, and a driver was apt to be a little upset if he emerged from underneath the engine covered in ash.

Churchward's Mogul 43xx Class, as in Chapter 6. The 'Maid of all Work' and forerunner of the "Halls", "Granges" and "Manors". Wonderful locomotives with boiler pressure of only 200lbs and a tractive effort of 25,620lbs, they were grossly overworked and overloaded, but then would respond to every type of work demanded, be it express passenger or heavy freight. Note reversing lever in mid-gear, the correct way to leave a locomotive.

No 2327 *Trevithick*. Mr. Billington's Class 'Remembrance' of the old London, Brighton, and South Coast railway, For a Great Western fireman to remember this class with affection is credit indeed, they were magnificent engines. Chapter 2 and 3 describe my feelings well enough, somewhere in the background of their design there 'MUST' have been a Great Western man.

Great Western Tank engine No. 5240 seen here at Reading sheds in 1953.

No. 7204 Tank engine. A stretched version of the 52xx Class (as described in Chapter 7). They were an immensely strong engine, in effect a 28xx with side tanks nailed on. All the big tank engines illustrated were designed for goods working, and guaranteed to remove the skin from firemen's knuckles. During hot weather the fireman's sweat kept the coal dust from flying.

Note position of guide on the reversing lever just visible behind the nameplate of 6924; she is linked up to 25% cut-off giving maximum economy in running, evident from the excess steam from the safety valve. It is said that Mr. Stanier 'poshed up' the 'Hall' class on the L.M.S. and called it the Black 5.

No. 4900 *Saint Martin*. This engine was the first of the 'Hall' class, which was to become one of the most versatile class of locomotive ever built for the Great Western. *Saint Martin* was a beautiful engine to work on.

No. 8457 Stanier class 8F of the L.M.S. The point I like about this photograph is the small oval plate that can just be seen over the buffer. Bolted on the frame it read 'Built at Swindon for the L.M.S.' This was the modern version of the 30xx class. Adopted as the R.O.D. engine, Great Western enginemen found them to be fine engines, they had to be, they were designed and built by an ex-Great Western man. One thing new to us was a door fitted each side of the cab between engine and tender, a refinement missing on a Western engine. Was it perhaps that L.M.S. men were in the habit of falling off?

No. 3283 *Comet* of Chapter 4. One of the remaining 'Duke of Cornwall' Class, she had a sister engine at Didcot, No. 3254 *Cornubia*. No wonder those Yanks thought she was the 'General Grant'. Note curved splashers, narrow cab, small spectacle type cab windows, almost impossible to look through. Like the driver in this photograph, it was preferable to place one hand on the brake lever, one hand firmly on the cab side, and look round the corner. When these engines were running at speed, it was a sight to see those great side rods going round. the boiler pressure was only 180lbs but they would run with the wind.

No. 6000 *King George V*. The 'King' herself, as I knew her (chapter 6), was without the double blast pipe which she now has fitted to her. She was also in her original condition as built. To ride on a 'King' was as near to riding on a turbine as one could get on a steam engine, the power was almost unbelievable, you opened the regulator and it responded immediately.

No. 4702. Just a handful of these engines were built by Mr. Churchward in 1919. To step up onto the high footplate of one of these engines was almost the same as onto a 'King' but with a small cab. They were popular with enginemen because of the sheer all out power and running qualities, but firemen found them to be the 'coal minder's' friend. On the occasions I fired them I found there was not much time to sit down. Built for express freight trains they excelled, but they could also be run hard and fast on passenger trains. Notice the steam blowing from under the footstep in this illustration showing the left hand exhaust injector working.

The 'Grange' illustrated is No. 6854 which was a class derived from the 'Hall', as were the 'Manors'. All were very fine engines; the Grange class were most notable for their free steaming. The pipe hanging from the cab of No. 6854 is the coal watering pipe, known as the 'pep pipe' to loco-men.

No. 3284 *Isle of Jersey*. Another of the 'Duke of Cornwall' Class. Note the larger cab and absence of top feed. Twenty years separate the two photos, as can be seen in the method of 'engine cleaning'.

Eastleigh Yard, then orders to take the engine to Shed, leave her there and return home.

My Mate had relations living in Southampton, so he went off to visit them, leaving me to make my own way home. It was an opportunity not to be missed. Here was a Great Western Fireman, for once with time on his hands on a large Southern Shed, and in those days Eastleigh Shed was full of every type of locomotive they had.

I knew if I just wandered round on my own I should soon be spotted, so to avoid any trouble I reported to the Shed Foreman and explained the circumstances to him. I told him how we on the Great Western had the "Remembrance" Class, and what fine engines I thought they were, and how much I would like to look round the Shed.

That Foreman was kindness itself; he gave me a free hand to go where I liked. The obvious first choice was to the "Merchant Navy" class *Channel Packet* being prepared for the road. She was a beautiful locomotive, even if the Fireman did refer to her as a 'spam can' but he was proud of her, even as I was proud of our "Kings" and "Castles".

The two parts about her I did like were the electric lights in the cab and the steam pedal for operating the firebox doors, but I could not work the pedal with comfort when trying my hand with the shovel, for the engine was left-hand drive, which to a Western Fireman used to right-hand drive meant firing 'cockie handed' or about-face. But what a firebox, it looked big enough to steam the *Queen Mary*!

One part of her I should have to remember to tell my Mate about, was the absence of a flare lamp. The Southern Driver took round with him an electric inspection lamp, and simply plugged it into points on the frame. I should have liked the chance to fire her on the road, but it was not to be. After a good look round I reported to the Shed Foreman again and thanked him for giving me the chance to look round his Shed.

He walked with me to the top of the Shed, and in our conversation he pointed to a sand bin in the corner of the Shed. It was kept there usually full of sand to deal with incendiary bombs. He told me that a few weeks previously he had been caught outside the shelter during a heavy raid, and he had dived into that sand bin for protection. The funny part about it was that he was on the large side and the bin was not all that big, and he had since tried to get into it again but without success; such is the incentive for self-preservation.

I made my way home with much to think on, but nothing would shake my faith in the Great Western engine. We might not have steam-operated firebox doors or electric lights in the cabs, but we had the best engines.

Like all railways in wartime, we were grossly overloaded, but we managed to deal with whatever came our way. I used to marvel at the way the 43XX Class would handle a heavy goods train. Had Mr. Churchward allowed for this kind of work when he first designed them, or was it one up his sleeve for future requirements? The early built ones were unchanged when I had to work on them. We had three allocated at Didcot—4326, 5379, and 6397. They were kept in good condition by the Shed fitters, but 4326 was an outstanding engine.

The "Forty-Threes" we had on the road were not quite so good. They were not only 'common users' but were on the road for long periods without the care and attention they should have had. If any one of our three was missing, Bill Young would soon make enquiries round the Division to get it back.

Pulling out of the up gully at Didcot East Junction or from the west curve across Foxhall Junction were the places to see their brute power at work. As each cylinder took a charge of steam they would rock from side to side, for all the world like a ship rolling in heavy seas, but once they had got their teeth into the load and it was possible to link up a bit they would start to run. Like all the Great Western engines, on a firebox of good Welsh steam coal to bite on they would perform prodigiously, moving tons over the limit.

The end of February 1944 came, and with it my association with Jack. He was moving back into Number Four Link, which would give him a few more weekends to get home. I should miss him as I had missed all my Drivers when it was time to part.

A Driver and Fireman work very much as a team, each depending on each other and I had been very lucky, all of my Mates were good chaps. So who should I fall in with next? I knew I should have a short period spare. I never did find out how it worked, but there was never a clean change-over for the Fireman, he always kicked about the Shed on his own for a couple of weeks, but this time I was in for a surprise.

I followed the duty sheet down the list of names to see who or where I was booked for the next week, and when I found my name I could hardly believe my eyes, "1.45am Thatcham. Engine 6106. Driver: H.G. Gasson. Fireman: H.H. Gasson". I was to fire to the 'Old Chap' for a week! To see 6106 in Didcot Shed now, beautifully preserved by the lads of the Great Western Society, brings back many happy memories, not only because I worked on her with my father for a week, but because also I have worked her for thousands of miles. She is truly a Didcot engine, home where she belongs and in steam, not cold and silent in a museum gathering dust along with *Lode Star* and *City of Truro*.

The duty was a nice little round trip; leave Didcot yard for Thatcham paper mills, put off the wagons in the mill yard, then on to Newbury with the rest of the train; this dispensed with we would run down to Newbury race course, stand on the blocks over the turn-table until 8.00am, return to Newbury Town station, run a fast passenger train to Reading, then back to Didcot with a stopping passenger train.

On the outward journey we were routed up main line to Reading West Junction, then round on the Berks and Hants Line, so we could go sailing past the sluggards puffing away on the up relief.

The 'Old Chap's' policy was to drive only one way. He not only liked to keep his hand in with the shovel, but he used to say that if a Fireman was to become a Driver then the only way to learn was to let him drive. I soon found that he meant it.

We walked down the road to the Shed together not saying much. I think he was a little bit excited, as I was, at the thought of father and son working together. We prepared 6106 inside the Shed, then pulled outside and filled her tank.

I had cleared out all the large lumps of coal in the bunker in making up the fire, and had broken up the rest into small pieces so that it would pass through the hole in the cab. There is nothing more awkward when on the run with a tank engine than to find one's firing impeded by a large lump of coal jammed in the hole. There isn't room to swing a coal pick, and while one is poking, prodding, levering, and swearing to clear the obstruction, the fire and boiler are getting lower and lower.

We washed hands, made our can of tea, and then Father informed me that I was the Driver on the outward trip, and to show that he meant it he handed me his pocket watch, note book, and train journal. If I was going to drive then that did not mean just lift the regulator, it meant doing the lot. I was also informed that the big lever on the right hand side was not just for going forward and backward, it was put there to shorten the travel of the valves, and if he had to shovel more coal than was necessary then I would get a wet shirt when it was my turn to swing the shovel. Point taken.

We pulled out of the yard, across the junction and on to the up main line; I started to pull the lever back a bit at a time until she was on the last notch and almost in mid-gear. The 'Old Chap' looked up at me with a grin, and reminded me that I had a pocket watch and a note book, and it was time to get the pencil out and use it. I had forgotten all about booking. We swept along with the regulator just open until I sighted Scours Lane Distant on, then it was a case of shut off, lever into the 45 notch and let her run so that we took the junction at just the right speed; then, as we passed over the Oxford road bridge, open her out again and on to Thatcham and Newbury. We detached our half-dozen wagons in the yard, carried on to Newbury Town yard, then light engine to the race course for our breakfast. Father would be the Driver on the passenger work, and a good job too for I don't think I would have had the confidence to run 6106 to Reading like he did. That engine will run with the speed of a "Castle", but it is not the fast running so much as stopping at the other end, and that is what the skill of handling a steam locomotive is all about.

We ran into Reading No. 1 bay dead on time, but our lady passenger guard made a point of informing us we were half a minute late. Father looked down at her from the height of the cab, tilted his cap over his eyes, and in all seriousness told her that we had miscalculated the wind resistance of the two headlamps we carried on the front buffer beam! She strode up the platform quite satisfied with the explanation.

It was a wonderful week and one I shall never forget, and I found the answer to something that had puzzled me for a long time. As a small boy I had owned an air pistol, and with the aptitude of small boys I had become somewhat of an expert shot with it. Our garden backed on to the gardens of the houses on the other side of the block, and one day a neighbour was in his garden at the bottom of ours doing some weeding. The sight of that big backside was a temptation too great to bear; as he bent down I let fire from my bedroom window. He gave a yelp, put both hands on his backside, and looked round for the culprit. I was down under the window frame. The day afterwards my air pistol disappeared, never to be seen again, and I was wise enough not to make any enquiries about it. It was on the last trip with Dad and we were rattling along over the river bridge just east of Cholsey station when he came over to me and asked me if I remembered owning an air pistol. When I nodded my head he pointed to the river and told me that was where it had ended up. The 'Old Chap' had taken it to work and tossed it over the side. I gave him a grin and said it was better then having my block knocked off.

The next week my new Mate came into the picture, and with all respect to the other Mates I had worked with, Ted Hurle was the greatest man next to my Father. We hit it off right from the start; I was to have a wonderful time with him.

Dear old Ted, who gave so much pleasure with his company, and who passed away the day after he had retired.

6

Ted had come up from Llanelli Shed to Didcot but he was not a Welsh lad, having started out from the small village of Edington and Bratton, just outside Westbury; after service life in the Great War he had settled down in Wales and joined the Great Western.

Most of his firing had been on the 43XX Class, or the 52XX and 72XX Tanks; it used to grieve him to see how we carried on with the two big tank engines, but we were the victims of circumstance, and with every chance of there being hours between any water supply we had to take drastic measures to ensure we were full.

The 52XX Class had a capacity for 1,800 gallons in the tanks, the 72XX Class a little more with 2,500 gallons, but both were far short of the 3,5000 to 4,000 gallons we were used to, plus the fact that with the tank engines we could not top up on the water troughs, so when we filled up we also filled the boiler.

We would fill those tanks to the last quarter of a pint, but the boiler, (I look back on it now and shudder), was filled so full that it was a wonder that the cylinder ends were not blown off. Those pistons could no longer be propelled by steam, we must have been working on the hydraulic principle! The problem then arose on the first movement, and on no account could the engine be allowed to blow off or else she would blow water to the moon! The regulator had to be opened so carefully that she crept forward with just enough power to move until the water level in the boiler had dropped. This was the time for the piece of chalk to come in handy—no self respecting Fireman was without a piece of chalk in his pocket to be used on the water feed.

When the injector was put on the water feed handle was pulled open and the live injector handle turned on, then the water feed handle was tapped back towards the stop, while an eye was kept on the overflow pipe under the foot steps until any surplus water stopped running. The injector was then taking all the water, so we would place a chalk mark on the feed handle and also on the supporting bracket, then the next time the injector was used the feed handle would be opened only to the chalk mark. We not only saved a lot of water, but at night time it saved hanging over the side with a torch or the gauge lamp to watch the overflow.

We arrived at a sensible arrangement with these big tank engines. I would open the water feed to the chalk mark and Ted would give the live steam handle a turn, so we used every drop without waste.

If ever there was a man with a sense of humour it was Ted; he could laugh when other men would have given up in despair. One of his favourite parts of the Division was between Didcot and Reading, particularly when we had a "Forty Three" Class engine with the open cab. Ted, like my 'Old Chap', thought that the Fireman should take a spell on the regulator, so we would start off up relief to Reading and by the time we had reached Moreton we would be spanking along. This would be where Ted could start to enjoy himself. He would look back towards the up main line waiting for the first express to show, then as the train drew near he would go into action. With our train running at 45mph and the express at 70mph there would be several minutes where we would be running side by side.

In those days the corridors of the coaches would be packed, and passengers would watch with interest the working of the engine running along with them. Ted would go up into the corner of the cab, remove his cap, and place on his head a large coloured hankerchief knotted in each corner; he would then take out his teeth and place them in his pocket. He was now ready to perform. He would pick up the shovel and get stuck in, firing her with a great show of exhausting labour, then he would slide the shovel into the coal, stagger over to my side, place one hand on my shoulder and the other hand on the water scoop handle for support and start panting. Then he would remove the head-gear revealing a large expanse of skin, wipe off the perspiration, pick up the shovel and start firing again. I would be sitting on the seat all this time, with my arms folded and a very stern look on my face, and the second time he stopped firing and staggered over for another breather I would pick up the shovel, place it in his hand, and make gestures to him to get on with it.

The passengers in the corridor would be looking at me with loathing. That poor old man having to work like that while the young one sat there and watched him. When the train had passed us Ted would give a grin and say, "That's given the buggers something to think about!"

I used to think that one day someone would write to the Management about old men being exploited, but nobody wrote to the 'Times'. If they had done so Ted would have been delighted. One day, after this performance, a very large sailor dropped down the window and started hurling abuse. Ted opened his mouth and showed the sailor a row of pink gums in a caricature of a grin, so I took off my cap and cuffed him with it!

The sailor nearly went mad with rage. I thought we had perhaps gone too far with our joke, but we heard nothing more of it. Ted, however, could not stop laughing; I only had to take my cap off and make out that he was going to be cuffed again to start him off!

He used to tell me about his mate in the trenches during the Great War. They had gone through the lot together, but had lost touch over the years. Ted knew that his mate had joined the Great Western but did not know where, but when he told me his name I knew where he was; it was one up my sleeve to give Ted a surprise in a few weeks time.

This old mate of Ted's was a Driver at Winchester, named Tommie Keoghon. In a couple of weeks we would be working on the Branch, and I had worked it out that when we were working the 3.35pm Didcot to Winchester passenger we would change over trains with the Winchester goods on the Branch somewhere, and the Driver would be Tommie Keoghan.

Ted hadn't bothered to learn the road to Southampton, as he knew I had worked every inch of the line and knew it backwards; it was nice to know he had that much confidence in me.

It was worth holding on to that bit of information to see those two old mates meet again after so many years. We ran into Burghclere to stop opposite the engine on the Winchester goods; it was just a matter of stepping over the space between the two engines.

Ted looked over and saw Tommie at the same time as Tommie saw Ted. They just stood there for a moment not saying anything, then the penny dropped, there was a whoop of delight from both of them, they hugged one another, danced the footplate in each others arms, and completely ignored the whistles and flag-waving of the Guard. There was so much to say and no time to say it, but it was Monday afternoon and we would change over each day for the rest of the week so there was plenty of time to make arrangements for the future.

Ted really appreciated that surprise, but the pleasure was mine also. I had a Mate I would do anything for; we were a good team.

The Southampton supply trains really came into their own now, so hardly a day went by without our being on the Branch. The engine power was the good old "Twenty-Eight" or "Thirty-Eight", the American Transportation Corps engines, or the L.M.S. "8F" which proved to be a very good locomotive. The latter were all numbered from 8400 and bore a small plate on the frame which read 'Built Swindon', so that was something even if the tender proclaimed L.M.S.

We would run out of Winchester Chesil station and over Shawford viaduct to see on the Winchester by-pass the largest collection of armoured vehicles ever known. There were tanks, self propelled guns, and amphibious 'Ducks' nose to tail as far as could be seen, and on each side of the by-pass the tents and supplies for this great Army.

We carried every kind of weapon, from boxes of small arms ammunition to large calibre shells and depth charges, all in open wagons, and to look back along the train to see some of those shells, nose up, oscillating with the motion of the wagons made one wonder if we would ever arrive without the whole lot going up with a bang.

On one of those trips we arrived in Southampton Old Docks behind the Ocean Terminal building late in the evening, and just in time to coincide with an air raid.

We left our train in the sidings, but before we could make our way out of the docks the German airmen very unkindly blew a great hole in the rails. Ted and I spent the night under the tender watching the biggest bonfire we had ever seen as the dock buildings burnt down; then when it was all over we had to wait until the hole had been filled in and the track repaired before we could leave. We were on duty for 36 hours on that trip.

The run into Milbrook Docks had its hazards also, not so much going in as coming out. We would come through Southampton Central station, through the tunnel, and head for Eastleigh and home. Just outside the tunnel, however, was a brick retaining-wall so close to the cab that it was unwise to stick one's head out. At the top of this wall were some houses with very small back yards. They must have been small, because one lady living there would empty her tea pot over the wall and down onto the line.

She did just that one day, and as I was in the tender pulling some coal forward I had the contents of her tea pot right down my neck! Ted roared.

The old saying of he who laughs last laughs longest was to be very true. We had a train of empties on the return journey so were routed to Winchester Junction and over the new single line connection to Worthy Down and onto the Branch again.

We made signs of drinking when passing Whitchurch Box to let the signalman know that we were stopping at the end of the passing loop for water; not that we really required water, but at the bottom of the embankment was a smallholding, and the other lads in the link had told us that it was possible to obtain eggs and tomatoes there.

I climbed onto the tender and pulled the water column round—we might as well top up as we had stopped. Ted slithered down the embankment and through the wire fence. I watched him walk up a gravel path and disappear between two greenhouses.

He had hardly gone out of sight when he reappeared, running back towards the fence, and behind him came a large black labrador dog going like a greyhound! His tail was out straight, and a row of white teeth could be seen under his curled-up top lip, he was grinning in the excitement of the chase. Ted reached the fence first, and for a small man he did a vault that would have been a credit to an Olympic competitor, one hand on the top wire and over he came.

I sat on the seat helpless with laughter. One emptied tea pot was worth seeing Ted clear that fence!

We both agreed to keep quiet about the incident, as it was obvious that we were victims of the old 'con trick'.

After the 'D-Day' landings in Normandy we were very busy running troop trains from Newbury and Sutton Scotney to Southampton Docks, returning with the empty coaches for a second and third trip before being released. Then, as the advance built up, we had train-loads of German prisoners for either Newbury or Banbury.

It was quite a shock to see some of the early captures; the black uniforms and silver braid worn by S.S. men, they did exist after all. But as time went on we took no notice of them; they began to look a scruffy lot, not a bit of 'master race' about them.

The difference in guards on these prisoner of war trains was amusing. The American trains would have armed guards patrolling the corridors, but the British trains would have one guard sitting on a kit bag at the end of the corridor, his rifle standing in the corner behind him while he read the "Daily Mirror".

As the Allied advance pushed further into France we started to run Leave Trains from Southampton, and for once we were able to indulge in some long non-stop runs. These were usually from Southampton Docks to Banbury, where we came off and the G.C. engine would take over.

Although it had been years since the Great Central had been

lost in the formation of the L.N.E.R. it was still the G.C. to Western men and would remain so until British Railways came into being.

Ted and I booked on one morning in late September to prepare one of our Didcot engines, a Churchward Mogul 4326, for one of these leave trains. We collected our 10 coaches from the sidings and set off south, empty to Southampton.

We had a good run down with no need to hurry as the timing was liberal, but as usual when a good start was made we were in for one of those days where things start to happen.

As we drifted down the bank from Worthy Down a Hurricane fighter came in from the south towards us, banked over our head, and dived down on to the Naval Air Station behind and started to fire his guns. The return fire from the aerodrome was too late to hurt him, but he climbed out of his dive, banked over and came back towards us. As he passed overhead we could see that our "Hurricane" was in fact a Messerschmitt 109; he had no black cross underneath, which we thought was a bit unfair. When he made a long low sweep to the east we could see that he was turning and coming back. Ted and I both thought that if he had any ammunition left he might take a crack at us—it was time to get a move on.

Now the drop down into Kings Worthy is 1 in 106 so we were beginning to move when we sighted the signalman. He was standing on the platform with the token all ready to make a hand exchange, and expecting our speed to drop. All credit to him, he stood his ground when he saw that we were not going to slack off. I lobbed the Worth Down token onto the post, and snatched the Winchester one out of his hand — in fact he was almost on the point of dropping it but I caught it just in time; we must have been touching 70mph. I looked back to see him bent forward against the wind pressure of our passing, then we were in the protection of the cutting. We were still way above regulation speed when we hit Winnall gas works siding; our old 4326 gave a lurch, then we were in the tunnel, the flanges of the engine wheels squealing in protest as we took the curve. Ted was braking hard, but we shot out of the tunnel and almost ran past the signal on Winchester platform.

The Winchester signalman said that he had just had time to acknowledge 'Train on Line' on his block instrument and book the time when we shot out of the tunnel. It was the quickest time ever between Kings Worthy and Winchester, but then, we had had an incentive to push that old engine along. I rang up the Kings Worthy signalman to see if he was all right. He was, of course, but a bit shaken. I see him sometimes now, and he still talks about seeing the great engine thundering towards him that morning. The Messerschmitt 109? We never did see him again, but we both felt a bit exposed as we rounded the curve of St. Catherine's Hill and swept over the long Shawford viaduct. The Observer Corps had nothing on Ted and I as we searched the sky!

We ambled along to Milbrook Docks, uncoupled along-side a ship, ran round the coaches, coupled back up again, and waited for our American friends. It was time for a brew up. After I had poured Ted a cup we had a good omen for the return run. Ted stood his tea on the tool box to cool, where it was bombed from a great height by a seagull. The top of the tool box looked as though it had just been painted white, except for a small circle where Ted's cup had been!

Although I washed that cup out with boiling water and steam, Ted refused to drink out of it again, so we had to share my cup. It proved a point, however, as I explained to Ted—a seagull has a tighter turning circle than a Messerschmitt, but Ted's indignant answer was that it was a British seagull not a bleeding German one!

While we waited for the American troops to board, the guard and the officer in charge came up on the footplate. There was a good deal of laughter when the story of our dash for safety was told, then we pointed out a hazard on the coach behind the engine. We had no blank on the corridor. The guard said he would lock the sliding door so it would be safe enough, then they both walked back to the guard's compartment, the American officer stopping to have words with two cigar-chewing American soldiers sitting in a Jeep. They tore off into the Docks to return within a few minutes with an enamel jug of steaming coffee, 500 Camel cigarettes, and a box of biscuits. They handed it all up to us with the compliments of the captain. The situation was typical of American generosity.

We chuffed gently away from the quayside and out of the docks, round the corner where it rained tea leaves, and headed north with plenty of time. We were not booked much faster than a goods train, so it was just a question of setting the regulator and letting her take her time. I took the token at Shawford Junction by hand and again at Winchester, but when we got to Kings Worthy it was in the bracket of the pick up post. I shouted

"Windy!" as we passed the signal box and received two fingers in reply. I think that the down trip had put the signalman off us somehow. It was a good run to Newbury, then we had to open up a bit as the timing was much tighter to Banbury. It seemed no time at all and we were sweeping down from Upton and clattering over Didcot East Junction heading north to Oxford. For once we had a clear road through Oxford. Ted and I were enjoying the run, but we were both getting a bit anxious about the water. We had started out with 3,500 gallons but we should make the water troughs at Aynho all right. Every now and again the corridor door would slide back, and an American serviceman would stick his head out, then finding he could go no further the door would be shut. Our Guard had evidently forgotten to lock it, but *we* both forgot to check that door at Aynho—the last person had left it open.

Ted took the water troughs fast. We needed 3,000 gallons to fill the tank, and I wound down the scoop and watched the level indicator climb up the gauge; as it neared the "Full" position I started to wind the scoop back up again, but our speed was too high, and the scoop too low, and I could not budge it. We were only half-way across the troughs so we knew that we could be in for a drenching. We therefore lifted up the running plate between engine and tender, so that any water gushing out of the vents would now run down into the track. But we had forgotten about that open corridor door.

At the 3,500 gallon mark the water lifted the tender flap and it went up in the air like a Texas oil gusher. Then wind pressure caught it and drove it through the corridor door and into the first coach.

When we ran into Banbury station we had run non-stop from Southampton. I climbed down onto the platform, then down between the engine and coaches to uncouple, as the G.C. Engine was waiting to take the train on.

I did notice a little water seeping from the coach door on the platform side, then I remembered about the missing blank on the corridor end. I climbed back up onto the platform and had a look inside the first coach. Our American passengers were sitting with their feet up on the seats; there was about six inches of water all through the coach, and any article left on the floor was swamped. But worse was to follow. A hulking great American marine was sloshing his way up the corridor with an automatic rifle clenched in both hands across his chest; he was making a lot of noise, and saying how he was going to shoot those "Goddammed engineers". It was time to depart friends, and in a hurry.

A Messerschmitt on the way down, a seagull when we got there, and a blood-thirsty marine at the end; we had had enough for one day! We dropped in Banbury Shed, turned 4326, and made for Didcot light engine. It had been a long hard day.

The week after, Ted was away on his annual week's leave, but I had no respite from the Branch. I was covering a Fireman who was also on leave, working the 3.35pm stopping passenger to Winchester, changing over en route, and returning with the goods. It was a good week although I did miss Ted, except that on the Saturday I had the biggest fright of my footplate career.

We were coming back from Newbury where we had been made up to a full load. The engine was 2226 and one I had fired for many miles; she was a Didcot engine and no stranger to either of us.

It had been a bit of a struggle from Hampstead Norris up the long drag to Churn, but as soon as she stuck her smokebox downhill for Upton the work was over.

I screwed down the tender handbrake, felt the blocks begin to bite, then placed my foot on the back plate and screwed the brake down as hard as I could. It was a long drop down into Didcot and with that heavy load we would have to be on top of it right from the start.

My Mate began to give her a bit of steam brake, and with each application I was able to give another quarter of a turn on the tender brake. About a half a mile down the bank my Mate made a full application of the steam brake. She held for a moment, then a loud bang came from underneath the footplate. The steam pipe had blown out, but this time there were no stop blocks to hit as I had done with Jack Thomas the year before. As we passed under the three arch bridge it was obvious we had lost the train; she was rapidly gaining speed. We rocketed through Upton, bucking and swaying over the crossover, the tender brake blocks were glowing red, showering a stream of sparks which tumbled and swirled away under the wagons. We blasted away on the brake whistle alternating with the train whistle, a frightful, urgent, desperate sound to be lost in the thunderous roar of the run-away train.

Upton signal box was just a flash of soft light and blurred windows with the silhouette of the helpless signalman at the window. Between the starting signal and the public stile the brake whistle snapped off at the stem, hit the boiler casing, bounced down onto the frame, and rolled down the embankment.

It was time to take drastic action. My Mate wound her into reverse and gave her some steam, and her free running changed almost at once; she began to labour and groan. As he opened and shut the regulator I worked the sand levers back and forth. She was beginning to respond, her speed was falling, but we were tearing the very heart and guts out of her.

My Mate placed her in mid-gear so that she ran a little sweeter, but as we passed the distant signal for Didcot East Junction it was obvious we would not stop at the home signal. We had one more course of action to take to try and stop her mad rush to disaster; we would have to abandon her. We both climbed down on to the bottom foot step on each side of her. As I let go and hit the ground I tumbled over and over hearing the wheels of the wagons clattering past my head. I picked myself up and ran along side the train, lifting up and dropping down the hand brakes on the wagons as they passed. Somehow, my Mate had also survived the jump and he was just ahead of me dropping down brakes on the other side.

As the brake van passed us we could see the Guard swinging into his brake with both hands, the blocks squealing in protest. But she was slowing rapidly; we had won.

We walked up the now stationary train to find the engine standing quietly near the home signal. I went to the telephone to let East Junction know that the emergency was over, then climbed back on board. My Mate would not move her with only the tender hand brake in use, so he made out a 'Wrong Line Order' form and I walked to East Junction Box with it. They were a bit shaken up in the box to receive the 4–5–5 ('Train running away on Right Line') on the block bell from Upton, but obeying Regulation 23 they had stopped all traffic until I had telephoned in. The signalman countersigned my 'Wrong Line Order' form, then I walked over to the station pilot engine with it and gave it to my old mate Jack Thomas. We went back up the wrong line, coupled up to our train engine and pulled engine and train into the yard at Didcot North, then 2226 was drawn back to the Shed.

Both my Mate and I were shaken up. I could not stop shivering, but a hot cup of tea in the engineman's cabin with a Woodbine soon had me feeling better. It had been a nasty half an hour and not one I should want again, although had it been in the daylight it may not have seemed so bad. Standing on the bottom footstep and then letting go had been the worst bit.

The next day we booked on for the same job, changed over trains again at Burghclere with the Winchester men and onto 2226 again. The return load was not so heavy, but when we stuck her nose down that bank at Churn it was with some misgiving; we both had our fingers crossed when we applied the brakes, but this time it was all right; it always is, but there is one time at least in every engineman's life when the moment of truth comes. You win some and lose some, and we had been lucky.

The Newbury line is now lifted, only the earthworks remain, but somewhere down the embankment past the position of the old distant signal is the brake whistle from 2226. I know to within 200 yards where it should be, and if circumstances allow it I shall return one day with a metal detector and find it. Polished up and mounted on an oak stand it will remind me of a day in the life of a Didcot Fireman.

Ted returned from his holiday and was most upset to hear of the run-away incident. He said that he couldn't leave me for just a week without me getting into trouble, but he knew what a run-away is like, as he had experienced one a few years before when he was firing. A 52XX Tank with a full load of coal wagons had got the better of him and his Mate, and they had landed up on their side at the end of a sand drag, with three wagons in the street below.

Before the winter set in, however, we were to have three wonderful runs. The first one started out innocently enough—we ran a battered old 43XX Mogul to Swindon for shopping, then reported to Control for orders.

There was a de-railment at Chippenham, and an empty coaching stock train for Westbury on the way from Gloucester to be run via Reading West and Newbury. We were ordered to relieve and proceed.

The train ran up the middle road and stopped. We licked our lips in anticipation—ten coaches and at the head 4045 *Prince John*.

The "Twenty Nines", "Forties", "Castles", and "Kings" were the only locomotives fitted with a speedometer, so we enjoyed our occasional run on them for the pleasure of that one instrument, and it was one of those days that Ted and I enjoyed; we were both in the right mood to have a go. Thank God the powers-that-be turned a blind eye now and again. It was not often we had our hands on a main line "Forty" in 'good nick', and she was in perfect condition, nicely warmed through from her run from Gloucester.

Ted eased her away, letting her take her time to build up speed, and as we passed under Stratton Park bridge she began to take on that long, easy stride of the greyhound she was. The speedo began to wave back and forth—30, 35, 40, 45. I put on the exhaust injector and began to fire her, the exhaust turning colour with each shovel-full, the distintive pungent aroma of good Welsh steam coal burning drifted back into the cab, and the pressure stood still at 225lbs, with just a wisp of steam from the safety valve.

At Shrivenham she began to run, Ted had set the regulator with the second valve just open and cut off at 30%. He wound her back half a turn to 25% and snapped down the reverser clip. It was now a case of letting her run, but run is not the right word, for she began to fly, speed climbing slowly from 70 to 75 mph. Between Uffington and Challow she touched 80, and the 'ton' was in sight. We slipped through Challow station so fast it was like the passing of the wind. We were in trouble now, as speed was far in excess of wartime running, but we had to get away with it. Mr. Churchward would have understood; it was as if he was there with us, as she kept climbing until the speedo wavered between 85 and 90mph. I had both hands on Ted's shoulders watching that needle, and it was with surprise that I saw him reach over and shut off. We were through Steventon and running too fast to go through Didcot without someone reporting us, and it was time to drop down.

We had all the distants off through Didcot, but Ted let her run to Moreton before opening her up again. We ran at a steady 60mph until he shut off at Scours Lane, then we drifted sedately round the corner at Reading West and headed towards Newbury.

I began to fire her more frequently now. She needed more to bite on for the drag up to Savernake, but Ted did not punch her for she was a lady even if the name-plate was masculine. I topped up the water on Aldermaston troughs as she settled down to a steady 60mph then sat down as far as Newbury to enjoy the running.

We swept majestically through Newbury middle road, and at Enbourne Junction we gave the signalman a toot on the whistle; for once, we were not turning left for Winchester.

At Bedwyn I fired her for the last time, for she would go to Shed at Westbury, and fire droppers do not appreciate a firebox full of glowing coal. As Ted shut off at Savernake, I closed the exhaust injector, opened the firebox doors and sat down. I could now enjoy the long sweep down through the Wiltshire country-side.

Ted came over to my side as we ran down through Edington and Bratton, pointing out places he had known as a boy. It was a scene worthy of a painter, the green of the fields, the russet colour of the trees, and this beautiful green and copper-topped locomotive gliding down, a blue haze just visible from her chimney, a feather of steam whisking away from her golden safety valve, and the quiet echo of her vacuum pump slapping away. We could have gone on for ever, enjoying the sheer beauty of that moment. If ever there was a heaven for enginemen then this surely must have been it.

Regretfully we climbed down from her at Westbury. For a short time she had not been a Great Western-owned engine but was ours, and she had given us a gift that would remain forever, long after the passing of steam; she had given us perfection between man and machine.

We had for once enjoyed a high speed run, even if it was only for a short distance. That 90mph between Challow and Steventon would never be recorded except in our memories, and we would never again have the same chance. For one brief moment of time we had experienced immortality. The sedate pace of 60 for the remainder of the run was just routine running.

We did the next year run 2915 *Saint Bartholomew* up to 95mph but that was 'light engine' and she was so rough on her boxes that it was impossible to fire her after she had reached 75mph so we never did touch the 'ton'.

Early November was to see Ted and myself engaged in another run of some distinction—distinctive to a couple of goods men anyway. We booked on duty at 8.00pm, relieved the crew of the 1.15am Aberdare to Old Oak Common at Didcot West Box and set off in fits and starts for London. Our engine was 3822, and she had been on the road for 19 hours so was past her best. However no running was required, as the fog was so thick we could not see her chimney and it was just a question of "keep moving". We crept from signal to signal all the way to Reading, with distants on and the A.T.C. buzzer sounding each time we hit the ramp. It was a miserable journey, both of us were chilled through from leaning out of the cab to find the home signals, and neither of us were looking forward to the approach to Old Oak Common. The country fog we could bare with, but London fog was another matter; it was so thick and clammy you could almost walk on it. How the Old Oak men could put up with it I could never understand, but thank heaven for A.T.C., at least we could run with confidence when the distants were off and the bell was ringing in the cab.

At Reading goods yard we topped up the tank, as speed over Goring troughs had been too low to pick up water, but that short stop gave the train in front of us a chance to get away. We pulled up through the station and received our first bell with Twyford distant off; it was to be a clear run to Slough, then we caught up with that train and the pattern was repeated until we pulled into Acton Yard. It was 4.00am, we were tired out, eyes red-rimmed with the constant searching for signals. We left the train and groped our way on to the ash pit at Old Oak Common Shed, then climbed down from 3822 and made for the warmth of the enginemen's cabin. It was time for a cup of tea and a chance to relax for a while,

When the Shift Foreman came in we reported to him, and as we had been on duty for eight hours he told us to make our way home. We walked over to the carriage sidings and caught a lift to Paddington in a train of coaches, arriving just in time to catch the 5.30am. As we walked up towards the engine we saw the Fireman climb down holding his hand, and from the look on his face he was not too happy. As we drew near we could see why, the blood was dripping through his fingers onto the platform. He told me he had crushed his thumb when the tool box lid had slammed down on it. I told him to go and get some attention to his injured hand, and to inform the Locomotive Inspector that the Didcot Fireman would see the train through to Swindon.

Looking over his shoulder I could see the number of the engine – 6000 *King George V*. Didcot men never had the chance to work a "King" for they were all stationed at Old Oak Common, Wolverhampton, and Laira, and as tired as I was I did not intend to miss this chance if the Driver would take me.

Ted had never been on a "King" either, so we both climbed aboard, and with departure time one minute away the Driver was most pleased to see us. I can remember that his name was also Ted, and that he was a very small man, in fact when he sat on the tip-up seat his feet dangled underneath. So we had on the footplate two small Drivers to one very large engine, with a tall lanky Fireman in between.

Ted looked back along the train to catch the 'right away' from the station staff, while I placed the shovel in the firebox to deflect the smoke and gasses so that I could examine the fire. *King George V* had a perfect fire prepared by an expert. Boiler pressure was just below blowing off at 250lbs and the gauge glass was full; she was as ready to receive the attentions of a country boy as she would ever be. I looked into that great 11ft.6inches of firebox, and began to wonder if I should ever ring the bell on the front framing.

There is a story about ringing that bell. It has been suggested that if a Fireman could throw the coal hard enough to reach the front end of the Firebox it would ring the bell, and to some extent this story was true, but only for the benefit of young Cleaners and Apprentices at Swindon Works. They would be victims of a leg pull. The bell would be rigged, a long length of string being tied between the clapper and the damper handles, passing along the framing into the cab. A Cleaner or an Apprentice would then be invited to try his luck in throwing a shovel-full of coal up against the front end of the firebox, but try as they could they would not be able to ring the bell. Then of course the Fireman would show them how to do it; he would loop his left foot through the string, then as he swung round to place his shot up the front end, his movement was to get the audience to watch the coal going in the clang just as the coal hit the firebox front. The object during this movement was to get the audience to watch the coal going in the firebox so that they could see for themselves that there was no dirty work afoot, just as long as they didn't see that length of string.

I wonder if the lads at Hereford have ever tried it now that they have *King George V* in their care.

Dead on time at 5.30am my Ted gave Ted No. 2 the 'right away'. I looked up from the firebox and saw that we were in the presence of a 'master'. Ted No. 2 was a "King" Driver all right; he had donned a dirty old black beret, and placed over his eyes a pair of motor cycle goggles, then he lifted the regulator up about two inches, and *King George V* glided out of Paddington as if she was powered by electric.

I walked over to my Ted, placed one hand on his shoulder and had a look out. I could see along a massive boiler, long and fat-looking after our usual nondescript "Forty Threes" and "Twenty Eights", and on top of this great boiler was a squat chimney exhausting with a crisp sharp bark so characteristic of the Great Western engines; then we were into the fog.

Fog, I had forgotten all about it in the excitement of climbing up on 6000, I would not have much time to worry about it, for I would be far too busy. The A.T.C. bell began to ring with regularity, Ted No. 2 gave her a bit more 'stick' and began to link her up, I put on the exhaust injector which picked up with that sweet familiar singing, and got down to the serious business of firing this famous "King".

My Ted stood up in the corner out of the way, now and again nodding his head for me to look over at Ted No.2. He sat there swinging his feet under him, head stuck just round the corner of the cab, completely unconcerned with the fact that we were hustling along best part of 600 tons in a fog so thick it was like a solid wall, and on board with him were two men who had never been on a "King" before.

I fired her just the same as the "Castles", "Halls", "Granges", and "Manors"; under the firebox door, with the back corners packed tight, then straight down the middle. And she responded, holding pressure at 240lbs with the exhaust injector on, until we were passing through Slough, when she began to drop back a bit. I placed the shovel in the firebox and with the deflection I could see a hole in the fire on the right and left hand side of the firebox about half way up. I quickly filled both holes then looked round for the reason. The back damper and back middle damper were open as they should be, but the front middle had worked open, as it was not pegged down on the ratchet. This was attended to by wedging it shut with a piece of slate I had found in the coal. No more trouble from that quarter. She soon came round to 240lbs again.

When the buzzer on the A.T.C. went off as we hit the ramp for Reading east main it came as a bit of a shock. I had been so busy and so full of the novelty of firing *King George V* that I had no idea we were so close to Reading. With the nonchalance of the top engineman he was, Ted No. 2 eased himself off his seat, cancelled the buzzer and quietly closed the regulator all in one unhurried movement. He knocked down the reverser clip, wound her forward to the 45% cut off mark, let her run a few minutes, then gave the vacuum brake a short sharp burst. As the vacuum pump pushed the twin needles up again, he would give her another short burst. We dropped down in speed so gently one would have thought it was a clear summer day with visibility perfect. Then we were coasting into Reading down main platform with the fog swirling in behind us; one more application of the brake, this time a long one, and we were at a stand, dead on time.

He had a look in the firebox, patted me on the shoulder, then shut off the steam-heating to the coaches. All the slight leaks in the system on the train slowly disappeared and we could now see well back along the platform. Ted No.2 opened up the large ejector and blew off the brakes ready to leave, while my Ted gave me a Woodbine, pushed me up into the corner, and told me to stand well back; he didn't see why I should have all the fun, for he wanted to try his hand in firing a "King".

Whistles blew and green lights waved from back along the platform, so we gave a toot on our whistle and were off again.

Ted No.2 gave me a wink, and pointed at my Ted with the shovel in hand, then he opened up *King George V* full regulator and blasted her out of Reading.

The blast from the firebox was so fierce when my Ted bent down that he had to make a grab at his cap. Between Reading West main and Scours Lane Ted No.2 was still hammering her, and my Ted was shovelling as fast as he could and looking very unhappy.

Ted No.2 eased her down and wound the reverser back to 25% cut off, then he burst out laughing. It had been an incident he couldn't resist, one Driver taking the 'micky' out of another Driver, but in the nicest possible way. He had my Ted worried for a moment.

Ted enjoyed the firing as much as I had, but it was not all over yet, and as he was busy I wound down the scoop at Goring and filled the tank, then stood behind Ted No.2 to watch *King George V* at work.

The speedo stood at 60mph as if it was fixed in that position, without any alteration to the regulator or cut off. It was an example of controlled precision running that was the hall-mark of an ace engineman. This remarkable man just sat there with his arms folded, legs swinging, peering round the side of the cab. He would come back inside every now and again, pull out a battered old tin, roll a cigarette as thin as a matchstick, light it, then stick his head out of the cab again. Not once did he alter the setting, not once did he consult his watch, yet when we ran into Didcot we came to a stand again dead on right time.

Going up in the early hours Ted and I had been chilled through, but Ted was now glad to wipe his brow; free-steaming as that engine was, she still needed a lot of work to keep her going.

I handed Ted his jacket and picked up the shovel, only to have it taken out of my hand by Ted No.2, while my Ted was gently led over to the Driver's side and told to get on with it.

The grin on his face went from ear to ear. I had fired her, Ted had fired her, and now he was invited to drive her. And drive her he did, with all the aplomb of the other Ted. If my Ted had been a regular "King" Driver, he would have been a cracker of a main line express man. The way he handled that engine was a joy to behold, and Ted No.2 was his equal with the shovel. All together, for the three of us, it was a trip we shall never forget; we parted at Swindon, making promises to write and get together again, but we never did. He did seek out Bert Edmonds and tell him that his nephew at Didcot had now got the rudiments of boiling water!

We all had a cup of tea after being relieved, and travelled back up to Didcot as passengers, leaving Ted No.2 to carry on to Paddington. We would sometimes see him when on the road, and when that encounter took place the blast on the whistles would send the cows in the fields running.

That run was an example of Great Western locomotive comradeship, with each man ready to help out in an emergency, and the world was a better place for it. The end of steam was the end of a special relationship. How can a diesel engine compare with the living beauty of steam?

The third run to remember came in the first week of December, and was quite the opposite to the two main line runs.

We had a bad outbreak of flu at Didcot Shed, so Ted and I found ourselves covering a passenger link duty together, on the 7.37am Didcot to Southampton. On Monday and Tuesday we had Collett 2222 as motive power, and expected to have her all the week, but fate took a hand in our lives, plus the sentimentality of Bill Young the Shed Foreman. We were both walking away from the Shed between the coal stage and the carriage sidings, making our way home, when I glanced over towards the ash road. There was the usual collection of locomotives waiting for their fire to be dropped, but I could see a "Bulldog" half hidden under the banking and half of a word on her nameplate. All I could see was 'lark' but it was enough, Ted and I were round that banking in a flash, and there she stood, 3454 *Skylark* of my boyhood days.

She was not in the pristine condition of pre-war days, showing some signs of wear and age, but she was still the same old *Skylark*.

Ted knew of my affection for this engine, so the proposal I made to him had his full backing. Back to the Shed we went, knocked on Bill Young's door, and bowled in, with the request that could we please have *Skylark* on the Southampton tomorrow. The answer was "No". What did we think he was running, a locomotive Shed or a private locomotive hire firm? But he hadn't allowed for the eloquence of Ted, my Ted who was Welsh by adoption, talking to a full blooded Welshman. Had he no soul? Had he no romance?

Had working with the English driven out all that was held dear in the Valleys? Had he no compassion? He stuck it for some time, then he said "yes" to get a few moments peace before Ted started again. There had to be a reason for this impassionate speech by Ted, he had conducted this appeal with all the virtuosity of a great criminal barrister defending his client at the Old Bailey. So, after Bill had said yes, the next question was "Why? And it had better be good".

I related the story of years ago when this locomotive was my 'Old Chap's' regular engine, and how I held her dear to my heart. I was, in fact, beginning to pick up where Ted had left off.

Bill held up his hand; enough had been said, we could have *Skylark* tomorrow, and to show us both that under the bowler hat was a brain full of compassion we had alleged he was so sadly lacking, my 'Old Man' would be taken off spare duties for one day and booked "Learning the road to Southampton". I asked Bill if I should kiss him now or when we came back, then beat him in reaching the office door and the safety of the Shed outside. It was a beautiful little bit of skullduggery to brighten up those wartime days.

When I arrived home and told Father he was learning the road to Southampton in the morning with Ted and myself, his first reaction was that a mistake had been made. He had worked the Branch for 20 years and knew it better than either of us. Then the grey matter started to work; after all, he was the father of the son. Something was afoot and he tried every way to prise it out of me, but I was the son of my father; in skullduggery we cancelled each other out.

The next morning I was in the Shed long before Father woke up. He did not have to book on until 7.15am, just time enough to walk from the Shed to the station to catch the train, and in any case, I wanted to spend some time on *Skylark* apart from the normal preparation duties.

I had a look over the top of the brick arch before I started on the fire. Her tube plate had corks of clinker all over it, so I borrowed a tube rod from Ernie Didcock, the Chargehand Cleaner, and cleared her tubes, ramming the rod right through until it cleared the firebox end. There was evidence of a superheater seepage, but at least she would start with clean tubes. Ted arrived just as I was closing the smoke box door, and we set about getting her ready. Bill Young was a real old sentimentalist after all; he must have left orders with the night shift, for from somewhere they had scraped together a couple of Cleaners to give *Skylark* a wipe down—not cleaned as she had been in pre-war days, but wiped over with some oily rags so that she shone in the winter sunshine.

As we took water before leaving the Shed, I climbed along the boiler with an oily rag in one had and some sand in the other and gave the safety valve casing and her copper band round the chimney a good scouring. It was the finishing touch, she looked a beauty.

We backed on to the coaches in the bay platform and waited for Father, and as soon as his short familiar figure appeared up the station steps and headed towards us we both took up a position of studied innocence. Even then he didn't know what was going on. He climbed onto the footplate, and looked at Ted and me without saying a word, waiting for something to happen. Ted examined the finger nails on his right hand, blew on them, polished them on the lapels of his jacket, and then suggested that Harold senior had better have a look at the name plate of the engine.

The 'Old Chap' jumped down onto the platform and had a look. He turned round to us with an expression on his face that covered everything—surprise, wonderment, enjoyment, shock, and extreme pleasure, they were all there. He was at a loss for words for some moments, then he could only say two words, and for a man who did not use profane language those two words had a depth of affection, "You buggers, you buggers!" For once in my life I had taken the wind right out of my old Dad.

Ted said cheerio and disappeared into the first compartment of the coach behind the engine. Father, Son, and *Skylark* were reunited after so many years, but it was not to be the perfect run as planned. The years of neglect and age had taken their toll from that old engine, for all my efforts at cleaning the tubes, and even with a clean fire she was shy on steam. We had to nurse her like a baby, mortaging the boiler for steam on the banks, then letting her free-wheel down the other side to fill her up again, but we made it, having a wonderful day. Dad drove her to Newbury, I drove her to Winchester, then he took over to Southampton. We reversed the procedure on the way back. And Ted? He enjoyed the day of a gentleman, lounging back on the cushions watching the world go by!

Page 49 of Mr. R. C. Riley's *Great Western Album Number 2* shows a very fine photograph of *Skylark* on October 24th 1951, just before her withdrawal from service, and the poor old lady looks as if she has had enough. I regret now that I did not make a bid for one of her name plates, but she's gone the way of so many fine engines; far better to be broken up in the early days than stand for years in a scrap yard to be cannibalised for her brass and copper fittings.

The winter drew on, with the problems of severe weather. Most people think that a locomotive footplate was a warm haven on a cold day, but this was not the case. It was a cold and draughty place to work, the only part of your body to be warm were the legs when the firebox door was open for firing, and even then they were scorched. In an open cab the icy wind could be vicious; hands would split open with the constant contact with water, and to lean out of the cab in a driving snow-storm to exchange single line tokens was a pleasure to forgo at any time.

It was a time, too, when we had trouble with injectors. I've read of the "A4s" on the East Coast expresses having injector failures, (something that was unheard of with the Great Western injector), but in the winter we would have the water feed-pipe freeze, and there was only one answer to that. We would stop, wrap some cotton waste round the pipe, soak it in paraffin set light to it and hope for the best. It was a bit drastic but it never failed.

Ted, being a thin man, used to suffer with the cold, particularly his bottom, and each time we stopped he would open the firebox door, lift up his coat, and back up to the glowing heat. Then, as the heat penetrated and the smell of scorching cloth filled the cab, he would let out a long drawn out 'Ahhhhh' and quickly nip back to his seat and sit down to conserve the warmth. Being a young man I would pull his leg about it, but I am older now, and I too enjoy backing up to a fire. This method of warming is hereditary in the male, and all stems from Noah and his Ark; when Noah had a hole in his Ark he had to sit on it to keep the water out!

The suffering of Ted did not stop at the cold. He suffered from an insidious craving for gorgonzola cheese. I say insidious because I could not stand the sight of it, and the 'aroma'—phew! Ted, though, would eat it for every meal if he could get hold of it! I always knew when he had that cheese, because of the metal box. Normally Ted would carry his food in an old gas mask haversack, but when he had this gorgonzola cheese he would bring it in a little metal box. This box had a hasp and staple attached to it. Ted would place it on the floor boards in my corner, tie a peice of string through the staple, then tie the other end to the handrail. He would then place large lumps of coal all round the box, building up a wall between the box and me. I then would receive instructions to watch it, and if it moved I was NOT to hit it with the shovel, but to talk kindly to it, and coax it back behind the wall! What a great mate he was, never a dull moment with him, life was too short and it was to be enjoyed to the full.

His other talents were that of a matchmaker. Over the years I fired to him at every opportunity he would bring up the subject that it was time I settled down and got married, and that a very attractive young lady who worked in the Great Western Hostel would be a most suitable wife for me—and best of all, Boyo, she can cook like a dream!

He was right, of course, he always was. I met this young lady, courted her in the proper manner, and to Ted's delight married her. We have our Silver Wedding Anniversary in 1974, so Ted made an excellent job of matchmaking.

Ted and I stuck together until the end of 1947 when my seniority took me up into a higher link. Even on the last day together Ted refused to be down-hearted, but we were both upset. We had shared so much together, not once a harsh word between us, and if the roster clerk tried any move to part us during those years either Ted or myself was in to see Bill Young at once. The only time we were away from each other was at holiday time, for then we had no choice.

The shock was softened to some extent when I found who was to be my new mate. To say that the Lord moves in mysterious ways is something of an understatement; the vacancy for a Fireman in number two link was with a Driver I knew well, very well indeed. I was to be Fireman to Harold George Gasson himself, the 'Old Chap', the 'Old Man'. Father of the Son no less!

7

As Fireman to Father, household life took on some degree of sanity. Mother could arrange meals for all of us together, social functions could be enjoyed as a family for once, we both left for the Shed together, and returned home together.

We were both darts players of some standing in the London Division Staff Association, and playing together we were almost unbeatable. There was a time during this period that whenever the two Gassons walked into the Staff Association hut, or any of the local pubs, dart playing came to an end! We had wiped up all the opposition, and could not get anyone to play against us.

But it was more than father and son; as I had grown from boyhood to manhood the bond of affection between us had matured to a point where we knew each other's thoughts, and this bond reflected itself on the footplate. We both knew it could not last, for it was against Great Western policy to allow father and son, or two brothers, to work on the footplate together for any prolonged period of time. There was nothing personal about this, but it did reduce the possibility of the entire males of a family being lost in the event of any accident.

The only answer to this situation before the Management insisted that we were parted was to make the most of it. And we did. We ran trains as they had never been run before. The sight of the two Gassons walking towards a train to relieve the crew was the time for the local signalmen to look at the clock and begin to think of margins between the other traffic.

As soon as we 'blew up' for the signal the points would come sliding over, the signals would drop off one by one, and we would be given a run on the tightest of margins in front of booked expresses.

The signalmen knew us both, and could afford to take the chance for we wouldn't let them down. It was a wonderful time, but we did have a few cracks to put up with. Signalmen would lean out of the box windows and shout 'Fix!' or 'Wangle!', and our own shed mates would suggest good-naturedly that Bill Young wouldn't need to buy any cabbages for some time. But we accepted all the compliments with the Gasson grin, and got on with the job.

To the 'Old Man' I was just another Fireman. We worked

perfectly together, as we would have done with any other Mate. The only thing I had to watch was that I didn't 'bash' the engine when I was doing a spot of Driving, because if I did have a little go, when Father came to the Driver's side he'd drop the lever down a notch and say "Come on boy, it's my turn now, head down, backside up!" On the second week together we had the Incident of the cats and as usual this incident started from the most unlikely source.

The 10.30pm Banbury to Westbury goods had been brought forward four hours and routed over the Newbury Branch because of a de-railment at Southcote Junction. We booked on at 9.00pm and relieved her in the up gully at Didcot East Junction. The engine was 2858 and in fair-to-middling condition, in other words, she would steam her head off with the regulator shut and get a Fireman on his hands and knees praying up the banks in between the times he was standing on tip-toe trying to see the water in the bottom nut of the gauge glass. She was, in fact, the common run-of-the-mill goods engine. We had worked on better engines and worse engines, this was nothing new; the object was to get the best out of her.

The fire was a bit dead as she had been standing for a while, so I got out the long bar from the fire-iron rack and gave it a good lift up, then levelled it all over with the pricker. We now had a bed of fire to build on. I clambered up onto the tender, and with the light from the flare lamp picked out some nice choice lumps and threw them forward, while Dad Gasson built the fire up in Great Western fashion, right up to the firebox ring. On the back plate of the tender I found a fire bar. This went across the tool boxes, and then I shovelled coal forward until it was up over the boxes in a great pile. We should need it all before we closed the regulator at the top of Savernake bank.

I used the telephone to East Junction to let them know we were ready, and, as usual, when they heard my voice *they* were ready. The signal came off and the 'Old Chap' had started to move before I could get back onto the footplate. I waved the gauge lamp back and forth until the Guard answered with his hand lamp. We were complete. We gave a toot on the whistle to confirm, then we started to open her out for the long drag to Churn.

As the Banbury Fireman had predicted, she began to lose steam pressure, dropping back a little bit at a time, and without the injector on, but honour would not allow me to fail for steam with Father.

104

Halfway between Upton and Churn I had to put on the injector. The water level was dropping and with her head up hill I should soon uncover the lead fuseable plug. I began to get a bit concerned.

The 'Old Chap' came over and had a look. We had 120lbs of steam and quarter of a glass of water, but the fire was perfect even if the exhaust did sound a bit queer. Father solved the dropping steam pressure in his usual unconcerned manner; he placed his cap over the steam gauge, stood on his seat so that for once he towered over me, and said he would knock my block off if I had a peep under that cap. But it was obvious that all was not well at the front end, so we would stop at Compton, not for a 'blow up' but to examine the engine.

We eased down past the signal box and shouted to the signalman that we were stopping in the station to examine the engine, then as we came to a stand Father put the blower on, shut the firebox doors, and told me to open the smoke box. It was as he had expected, the jumper ring on the blast pipe was jammed on one side.

Twenty minutes were spent on cleaning that jumper ring with the sharp end of the coal pick, a couple of pocket knives, some cotton waste, and a few softly-spoken swear words, (although I did hear one loud word when Father lost some skin from his thumb). I filled the buckets of the signal box with coal, wetted the tea in the can from the signal box kettle, and had to admit that I still had something to learn about locomotives. Father knew what was wrong as soon as he heard the blast of the exhaust and the steam pressure began to drop, but he didn't think it would do any harm to let the 'Old Boy' sweat a bit! From then on 2858 steamed as she was built to. I had a job to keep her from blowing off and we ran all the way to Westbury without any more trouble.

The return trip was on a locomotive that was a favourite with all Great Western enginemen, one of the seven 4700 Class, No. 4701 that Mr. Churchward built in 1919. The chance to work on one did not come very often, as they were used between the West Country and Paddington Goods for most of the time. What locomotives, almost as big as a "King", they were just a little under the all-out power of a "Twenty Eight". They would run like a "Castle" on the vacuum fitted goods, and were used with some regularity on express passenger services. This one was not long out of Swindon following an overhaul. She ran so sweetly that each rail joint could be heard. It was my pleasure to drive her, as far as

Reading anyway, (as much as I enjoyed the regulator I did not fancy threading my way into Acton Yard). It was always the same when we had a free steaming engine; it was my turn to drive, while the 'Old Chap' sat there with firebox doors open and the engine blowing her head off. He used to say that the Devil looked after his own, but that was not fair, the Devil sat with him.

We put 4701 away at Old Oak Common Shed with just enough time to get up to Paddington and catch the 4.45am newspaper train home. The Driver had started to move before he saw us running, and being a good chap he shut off so that we could dive into the first vehicle, a parcel coach, and into the Incident of the Cats.

There was a distinctive and unpleasent smell in that coach, a heavy, clammy, and sickly smell that even outweighed Father's pipe; and that's saying something, because when he reached the bottom that old pipe sounded like a man in wellington boots walking on gravel! If we had to stick this all the way to Didcot then we were entitled to know what was causing it.

We tracked it down to a large wickerwork laundry basket. On closer examination there was no doubt; it stank, but not a sound came from it. There was no label evident to identify the destination. We discussed the possibility of a murder, it could be a body in the stages of decomposition. Two tattered straps and buckles stood between us and the answer; it was more than we could stand, so we undid the buckles and lifted the lid. It was not a body we had uncovered, but ten cats with one thought in their minds, escape—and before we could shut the lid they were out.

There then started a hunting expedition that would have done credit to a big game hunter. We used all the craft and guile, the sneakiness and cunning of the old time horse traders to catch those cats. The soft, sweet, calling of 'Pussy, Pussy' ended by the pussy being grabbed by the scruff of the neck and stuffed back into that basket, and each time a pussy was pushed in, another popped out.

Leaving Reading we decided we had caught them all, no more cats were to be seen. In the final check-round we found the label, "Ten Cats consigned to Kidderminster". It was agreed that we should make one more check. Father lifted the lid an inch while I shone my torch inside; twenty-two eyes glared back at us. We had them all safely back inside, down went the lid, and the straps were secured as the brakes were applied for Didcot.

Both of us were covered with perspiration and cat's hair, and we had worked harder in the last hour than all the night put together.

On the way home the 'Old Chap' suddenly stopped and asked me how many eyes I had counted in that basket, and when I said twenty-two he agreed. But the label had stated "Ten Cats", twenty eyes; where had the other two eyes come from? Father thought back on that label again, and remembered that it had read 'Ten Female Cats'. What if we had stuffed in a Tom with them? The consequences of such an action was too awful to contemplate.

When we opened the back door at home and walked in the old dog bounded forward to meet us with his usual greeting, then stopped short, turned round with a disgusted look and went back to his bed. He faithful masters had been consorting with cats! He was used to the smell of coal, steam, and oil, but this was the aroma of the enemy. We were duly punished, he ignored us for a week!

During this time with Father we relieved Uncle Bert Edmonds a couple of times, and of course he told Aunt Annie about it, and as Annie knew her brother very well nothing would convince her that it had not been a 'fix'. There had been some jiggery pokery between her Bert and her two brothers back in 1910, which resulted in them both turning up in Oxford, and although she loved them both she knew their capabilities; they were rogues, and her Bert was a rogue too for he had started it all with his brain-washing! Bert would suck on his old pipe and grin, he had heard it for years.

I think the situation did strike home one day at Reading. There was an engineman learning the road from Paddington to Swindon, and he had joined Bert Edmonds at Acton. Bill Gasson had relieved Bert at Slough, where the family news was exchanged, then the 'Old Chap' and myself had relieved Bill. All within two hours this poor man had been in the company of the Old Oak Branch, the Reading Branch, and now the Didcot Branch of the family! He was well aware that the Great Western was proud of the fact of being a family railway, but this was ridiculous! It was a situation Father relished.

A week later we had a Locomotive Inspector on the footplate with us. We were working a Divisional inspection special with 1334, the old Midland and South Western Engine kept at Didcot for working the Lambourne Branch. We stopped at Winchester for the top brass to take lunch, where the introductions were made; please meet Mr. Harold Gasson the Driver, please meet Mr. Harold Gasson the Fireman. Very important eyebrows were raised, very important heads were put together. As we climbed respectfully out of that inspection coach some very important muttering could be heard.

The Locomotive Inspector was most apologetic; he thought he was in the company of two Harolds, nothing more, but he knew as we did, the damage was done. We had got away with it for four months, and probably would have done so for much longer, but it was the end; a week later I had to exchange places with another Fireman, and with that exchange I would see the end of my firing days.

It was a quick and simple swop, Fireman Jones to Driver Gasson, Fireman Gasson to Driver Champ. Bill Young had us both in and explained the position. Orders had come from above. He was more upset about it than we were, but we had survived together longer than we had expected, and with Bill Champ as a Mate I had a lot to be thankful for.

Bill was one of those big burly men, and in common with men of his size he was as gentle as a lamb. He had one trick that used to amaze me with his strength; he would hold out two hands that were as big as a couple of shovels, catch hold of a Fireman in each hand—and I was usually one of them—and pick us up clear off the ground. He was full of practical jokes, and when he found I would jump if my knees were pinched it was fraught with danger to pick up the shovel! He would wait until I had started to swing with a full shovel, then make a grab for me. The result was coal all over the footplate. There was only one way to retaliate, and that was through his 'nose warmer'. The only time Bill was without his pipe was when he was eating. The stem was so short that it literally was a nose warmer, and sooner or later he would lay it down. I was all ready to 'doctor' it when he did so. I had cut a little rubber from the coal watering pipe, chopped it up fine, and had it all ready. I had to wait nearly a month before the chance came, and that was when Bill went to the stores, leaving his pipe on top of the reverser. I emptied out some of the tobacco, tipped in the chopped up rubber, then packed the tabacco back in.

Bill smoked that pipe-full without turning a hair—I think he even enjoyed it! His tobacco was like rubber anyway; he would cut it from a little black block, rub it in his hands and stuff it in his pipe. (It had its merits, for we never had a fly or wasp on the footplate, and if we were sent home as passengers we had the compartment to ourselves in a very short time).

Bill was of the same seniority as my Old Dad and his brother

Bill. They were all Firemen together, and I heard stories about those two that would fill another book, especially when they were all together in a double home lodge. For all the tricks I had got up to, I found that my 'Old Chap' in his time had been as bad!

The time spent with Bill was a happy one. He was an excellent Driver, in fact a good man to know and work with. I only saw him upset once.

We were spanking along on the down relief between Twyford and Reading on 7202, one of the big tank engines, when Bill sneezed and away went his beloved pipe, to bounce along on the ballast. Poor Bill was unconsolable. We were running much too fast to stop, and we could not stop in the section. Bill had his second-string pipe, of course, so he wouldn't be without a smoke, but it was only ten years old and by his standards just 'run-in'.

He hardly spoke a word for the rest of the day, so something drastic had to be done. We telephoned the signalman at Twyford and asked him to get the ganger for that section to have a look for the pipe when he walked through the next morning, then we set about making arrangements at our end.

The next day we put out feelers in the right quarter. The man in charge of the Control Office at Reading was Bert Povey, a Didcot traffic man who knew us both well. Now Bert Povey more than anyone else in the Division could appreciate the importance of that missing pipe, so with a little connivance on his part he had us relieve an up goods train at Didcot, work it to Reading West Yard, engine to shed, then orders to make our way home. He did not add "via Twyford", but the old saying "a nod is as good as a wink" applied here; we were off on the next up stopper to Twyford! That walk back to Reading was the only time I ever enjoyed searching a section. All enginemen at some time during the year search a section, usually for cattle on the line, or if a passenger falls out of a train, and always at Christmas time when some nit of a Christmas club treasurer finds he can't balance his books and throws himself over a bridge, so for a change we were not looking for bits and pieces of the human anatomy. We found Bill's pipe, a little battered about the bowl, but otherwise in good condition. The Great Western Locomotive Department could now breathe freely again, and Bert Povey collected a well-deserved pint in the Staff Association.

At the start of the summer we had a new duty added to the Didcot roster. A new goods train was formed to run from Moreton Yard to Feltham Yard on the Southern; we would work it to

Reading New Junction, then return light engine to Moreton for the second and third trips. It was quite a heavy duty for a night's work, around 110 miles of running, and to work this duty a request was sent out to the South Wales Divisions for three 7200 tank engines.

A request of this nature is manna from heaven to a Shed Foreman. It gives him a chance to get rid of some lame ducks, so the three 7200 Tanks we received were some right old tubs.

We received 7202, (the engine Bill had lost his pipe from), 7208, and 7228; out of the three 7202 was about the best.

Bill Miles, the Foreman Fitter, and his lads got stuck into them and made a very good job out of a bad bargain, but we disliked those big tank engines, I think simply because we were used to working on the open footplate of the tender engines so much. We had 6106, our own tank engine, but she was a Didcot engine and well looked after.

The 7200 Class were stretched-out versions of the "5200" tank engines, but to me they were "Twenty-Eights" with side tanks nailed on. Although the tractive power was slightly below the "Twenty-Eight" it would have been a good man who could find the difference; the power produced was sheer brute strength. It was most noticeable because of the lack of movement between any cab or tender. The "Seventy-Two" was just over 92 tons of solid dead-weight on the move, one great lump of steam locomotive pounding remorselessly on. This dead weight reflected in the way they rode, for there was no movement except forward, and the same applied, of course, when running bunker first. This was the whole idea of having them on this new duty, as it was basic economics to avoid the need for turning for the light engine trip back to Moreton Yard. Some bright boy on the management staff had worked it all out; let's bring in the "Seventy-Two" Tanks for this new duty, then we can get three trips each night out of the devils!

I only wished we could have had him on the footplate with us on a hot summer night, for firing those big Tanks was like working in an inferno; the heat must have put the temperature up to well over the hundred. We suffered, as we were gentlemen enginemen in the London Division, and not used to this type of locomotive. It was all right for the Welsh lads, they were brought up on tank engines. We changed our mind about them when the winter set in, for there was a sliding steel plate each side of the cab, and when this was drawn back we were cocooned in a warm little world of our own. We took back all that we thought of economic experts, (and at least they were Great Western engines, and anything Great Western was better than those Austerities!)

Bill and I did have one bit of fun that summer. We were running on the down relief between Reading and Didcot, and as we passed through Cholsey the signalman noticed that we had a wagon on fire about half-way back along the train. So he had us stopped at Aston Tirrold intermediate box, and the signalman there sent to Moreton for another engine to come on the up relief line and stop near the burning wagon and deal with the fire.

I rode back with this engine, taking our bucket with me. When we stopped at the burning wagon we could see that it was a wagon-load of farm manure. By this time the Station Master, Mr. Fouracre, had arrived from Cholsey, resplendent in a new uniform with gold-braided cap, and he set to work with enthusiasm. The object was to get to the heart of the fire, so he borrowed the coal pick from the engine, hit up the clips on the side of the wagon, and dropped the flap down.

This was excellent reasoning from a man of responsibility, but he had missed out one little thing, co-ordination, he hadn't informed me of his intentions as he dropped the flap on that wagon and poked his head over the top of that stinking burning manure. I was on the back of the tender with a bucket-full of water I had drawn up out of the tank, and at the precise moment that Mr. Fouracre stuck his head over the top of that manure, my bucket of water hit that manure about a foot in front of him!

Needless to say, the fire was soon out, but no farm worker mucking out a cow shed had ever got in the state that poor man was in. He was plastered in manure from head to foot. At arms length, we wiped him down with cotton waste, then stood him on the tender while we ran him back to Cholsey. We couldn't place him on the footplate near any heat, as he smelt bad enough on the tender! In later years when he was Station Master at Culham, and I was District Relief Signalman covering Culham Box for a day, he brought his wife out of the Station house and pointed me out as the only man to cover him with manure and get away with it.

I think that incident was the only time I have seen my mate Bill let his pipe go out. He started to laugh, and it went on for hours. He would go quiet for a little time, then it would cross his mind, and he would start all over again. There was more to steam locomotives than shovelling coal!

It was a good time, but the last few years of Great Western

steam were drawing to a close. Nationalisation was upon us, and with it the identification of being a true Great Western Engineman was to be lost for ever in British Railways. The locomotives were in need of repair and gradually getting worse, I had a talk with a Chief Inspector I knew very well at Paddington one day, and although nothing definite could be said, it was evident that with my seniority I could count on only a few years as a Steam Driver. I searched my soul for many hours before coming to a decision, but I did not want to be present at the end of steam; I wanted to leave as a Great Western Fireman, not a B.R. man.

The 'Old Chap' agreed with me. I had seen the best of the old days. His brother Bill's son, Ted, had just been made Fireman at Reading, so there would still be a Gasson firing in the Division. He told me later that it was a bad time when the decision was made to replace steam with diesels. The introduction of the Standard Engine softened the blow to some extent, but except for the brilliant work done by Mr. Sam Ells at Swindon, the common user engine began to fall rapidly into a state of disrepair.

The lads at Reading had some hairy trips out of Redhill with the old 4500 Class during the summer service in those last few months, but I think every man on the footplate at that time opened the eyes of those above; Great Western Steam went down with full honours.

I applied for a transfer to the Traffic Department as a Signalman. I had spent a few off-duty hours in the local boxes, and was fascinated by the work at the big junctions, so after a couple of weeks my application for a transfer was granted. I was sent to Reading Signal School for a three month course in signalman's training. My off-duty hours of study paid off; I passed the examinations and was out of the school in three weeks, and landed a Class Three Box at Milton. Three years later, and a lot of hours spent in study with the inevitable exams at the end, I was appointed to Class One District Relief Signalman, covering 22 signal boxes in the Didcot and Oxford District.

I think that probably the years on the footplate made me a better Signalman for they gave me an understanding of conditions and working of the steam engine that allowed me to operate a busy junction box much more effectively. The ordinary Signalman would wait for the Driver to blow up for the signal, but when I heard the ejector being opened I was setting up the road, and had the signal off before the whistle blew. Little things, but added together they made the working of a busy box much easier.

The Oxford lads soon got to know when I was at Kennington Junction. There was no need to hang the single line token from Cowley on the post, and they would sweep down off that branch at a speed no other Signalman experienced, holding up the token for me to take at the end window. I never missed—the Winchester Branch had taught me all about single line tokens.

Regrets? There were many, but if I have in this book re-captured some of the atmosphere of Great Western Steam, and the work of the enginemen, then all is not lost.

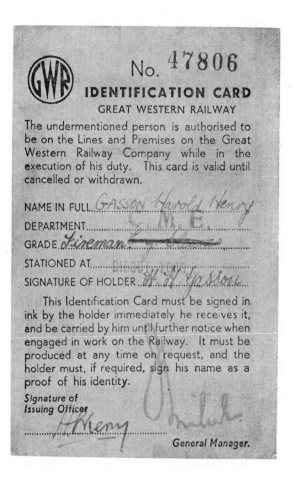